Retro Curved
PIECED QUILTS

15 THROWBACK DESIGNS
FOR TODAY'S QUILTER

ERIN GROGAN

Landauer Publishing

Retro Curved Pieced Quilts

Landauer Publishing, www.landauerpub.com, is an imprint of Fox Chapel Publishing Company, Inc.

Copyright © 2023 by Erin Grogan and Fox Chapel Publishing Company, Inc., 903 Square Street, Mount Joy, PA 17552.

Project Team
Managing Editor: Gretchen Bacon
Acquisitions Editor: Amelia Johanson
Editor: Christa Oestreich
Designer: Mary Ann Kahn
Proofreader & Indexer: Jean Bissell

ISBN 978-1-63981-034-5

Library of Congress Control Number: 2023944267

We are always looking for talented authors. To submit an idea, please send a brief inquiry to acquisitions@foxchapelpublishing.com.

Note to Professional Copy Services:
The publisher grants you permission to make up to six copies of any quilt patterns in this book for any customer who purchased this book and states the copies are for personal use.

Printed in China
First printing

This book has been published with the intent to provide accurate and authoritative information in regard to the subject matter within. While every precaution has been taken in the preparation of this book, the author and publisher expressly disclaim any responsibility for any errors, omissions, or adverse effects arising from the use or application of the information contained herein.

CONTENTS

INTRODUCTION, 4

TOOLS & MATERIALS, 5

TECHNIQUES, 8
How to Sew Curves, 8
Raw Edge Appliqué, 11
Daisy Dresden Quilt Block, 12
Big Stitch Quilting, 16

PROJECTS, 18
Rainbow Snails Quilt, 20
Peace, Love & Patchwork Quilt, 26
B-Side Quilt, 34
Darling Daisies Quilt, 42
Double Rainbow Quilt, 48
Marvelous Mushrooms Quilt, 54
Positively Pyrex Quilt, 68
Retro Blooms Quilt, 76
Strawberry Fields Quilt, 82
So Mod Quilt, 94
Retro Stars Quilt, 100
Setting Sun Wall Hanging, 108
Sprout Wall Hanging, 112
Mini Bloom Pillow, 118
Citrus Pillow , 124

TEMPLATES, 130

ABOUT THE AUTHOR, 157

ACKNOWLEDGMENTS, 158

INDEX, 159

INTRODUCTION

If you know me, then you know I'm a modern girl with a vintage heart. I like to blend the retro with the modern aesthetic. From this idea, I used some of my favorite nostalgic elements and motifs from the 1960s and 1970s and added my bold, modern touch to them. Some of my favorite elements are owls, snails, and of course flowers! These 15 different quilt designs evoke memories from the colorful retro era but are made for the modern home. The lines are clean and bold. The blocks are large and fun to piece together.

Since I was a young child, I've always been drawn to everything nostalgic about the 1960s through the 1970s. As a child during the '90s, when everyone was listening to their boy bands on their Discmans, I was rocking out to The Beatles, Boston, and Fleetwood Mac on my record player. The sound of vinyl is just magic. You can't convince me otherwise.

As an adult today, my love for this era hasn't changed. My kitchen is decorated in vintage gold, green, blue, and pink Pyrex®. My Pyrex collection was actually the inspiration for this book. There are 1960s swung glass vases on my mantle and pieces of vintage furniture here and there throughout my house.

Trends also have a way of repeating themselves. Lately, fashion and home décor have been pulling inspiration from the age of retro that I love. I've joyfully noticed midcentury modern furniture showing up in stores and friends' homes. Walking into the women's clothing department makes you feel like you've arrived at the disco: the colors are bright earth tones and the patterns are bold.

When designing these quilts there was one thing I knew for sure: retro art and design elements are notoriously made with soft, curvy lines. Incorporating sewing curves in my designs was a must. Therefore, you will find at least one curve element in each design. If you're new to sewing curves, don't worry. I cover three different techniques for sewing curves and provide lots of tips for making the process easy. Many of these designs incorporate different skills, like raw edge appliqué and making Dresden blocks. I also share with you my favorite techniques to achieve these design elements.

My hope for you, my new Quilty Friend, is that this book brings you joy. The nostalgic elements in each design can spark happy memories, like baking with grandma in her kitchen. If you don't love sewing curves yet, I know you will after working on a project from this book. It's important to me that putting a pattern together is a fun process, and I'm so happy you're going to be sewing with me.

~Erin Grogan

TOOLS & MATERIALS

The best advice I can give to any quilter is to invest in quality sewing tools. When we're working with the right tools for the job, a task can become much easier. Here are my tried-and-true quilting tools that I use every day in my sewing studio.

Sewing Machine: Forever my best friend in my sewing space is the sewing machine. All the patterns inside this book are machine-pieced patterns. Some of the patterns utilize raw edge appliqué. Because of this, you will benefit from using a machine that can do both straight stitch and zigzag stitch. I prefer to use the blanket stitch on my appliqué, but a zigzag stitch is a great alternative.

¼" (6.4mm) Presser Foot: My precision and piecing accuracy drastically improved when I started using a ¼" (6.4mm) presser foot with a guide bar. I even prefer this foot when piecing curves. A consistent seam is important when piecing together these patterns.

Decorative Stitching Presser Foot: Whether I'm topstitching my binding or appliquéing a small detail onto my quilt top, I always reach for my clear presser foot. I like seeing where I'm stitching when it comes to appliqué. You want to be sure the presser foot can also accommodate a zigzag stitch so that you don't break the needle.

50-Weight Thread: When it comes to piecing my quilt tops, I prefer a 50wt 100 percent cotton thread. You can choose coordinating threads or a good neutral like an off white or light gray. My go-to is always Aurifil 50wt color B311.

8- or 12-Weight Thread: When it comes to big stitch quilting, you can use either an 8- or 12wt thread. The 12wt thread is thinner than the 8wt and will blend into the quilt more. This is great if you want to add the extra texture of big stitch quilting, but you don't want the stitches to stand out. My go-to is always WonderFil® 8wt Eleganza™ perle cotton thread. You will always find bright balls of Eleganza thread in my travel sewing bags and a wall of them in my sewing studio. The 8wt is a thicker thread that can be used to add texture, pops of color, and contrast to your quilt. The 8wt is more visible and provides even more texture to a finished quilt.

Rotary Cutter: I like to keep both a 45mm and 28mm rotary cutter on hand when working on these quilts. You will find that the 28mm makes it easier to cut out the smaller curved pieces. I recommend changing out your blade between projects since a fresh blade makes cutting much smoother and reduces frayed edges.

Self-Healing Cutting Mat: The rotary cutter's best friend is the self-healing cutting mat. I personally favor one that is 24" x 36" (61 x 91.4cm) in size because it can accommodate cutting out larger pieces.

Quilting Ruler: If you're only able to invest in two rulers, I'd recommend getting a 6" x 24" (15.2 x 61cm) quilting ruler and a 6½" x 6½" (16.5 x 16.5cm) square quilting ruler. These sizes will be able to accommodate most quilting projects. My go-to are the Quilters Select rulers because they never shift when I'm using them.

Fabric Scissors: You will want to have a good pair of fabric scissors when cutting out the appliqué pieces. There are a lot of unique shapes that would be difficult to cut out with a rotary cutter. I'd also recommend having a small pair of snips for trimming threads and for cutting into the seam of curves.

Pins: Pins are a great tool for holding strips of fabric in place. I prefer to use thin pins with glass heads. They hold everything in place, and because they're thin, they slide into the fabric with little resistance.

Glue Pen: If you'd like to try the glue pen piecing technique (page 10), you will need a fabric glue pen. My go-to is the SEWLINE pen. It washes out and is easy to apply to small seams.

Seam Ripper: Mistakes are inevitable, but that's all right because we have seam rippers to unpick them.

Iron: To improve cutting accuracy, I'd recommend ironing all your fabric before cutting it out. Be sure you're pressing down with the iron and not moving from side to side. Ironing in different directions can stretch out the fabric fibers and warp the quilt block.

Fusible: There are many types of fusible on the market that work well for appliqué. For the quilts inside this book, I used HeatnBond® Lite. Since we're using the raw edge appliqué technique, I wanted to secure those raw edges as best as possible.

Starch: I didn't always sew with starch, but since I've started sewing so many curves, I've really seen the benefit in it. Starch helps to stabilize the fabric fibers, reducing stretching. This is important when piecing along bias edges, which is inevitable when sewing curves. Starch is also key in holding the shape of the Dresden blocks in the Darling Daisies Quilt.

Template: Every pattern in this book utilizes templates. It's important to confirm they're being printed at the correct size. I personally use paper templates, but if you're concerned about cutting into them, I'd recommend tracing your templates onto plastic template sheets.

Marking Tool: When it comes to big stitch quilting, I prefer to mark out my quilting design with a hera marker. I like that I don't have to worry about removing the marking later since it doesn't leave any marks on the fabric. Instead, it creates indents in the fibers. When it comes to tracing out my appliqué templates, I like to use a Pilot FriXion pen on the back of the fusible. Be sure to test out your chosen marking tool on a scrap of fabric before using it on the quilt to ensure it cooperates with the fabric.

Freezer Paper: You can find freezer paper at your local grocery store. It's a key tool when creating the shapes of the Dresden quilt blocks.

Clockwise (from the top): Sewing machine, thread, rotary cutter, marking pens, marking tools, pin cushion with pins, fabric scissors, cutting mat, quilt rulers, starch spray, fusible, and iron.

TECHNIQUES

All the patterns in this book use traditional piecing techniques. Some of them incorporate other techniques as well, such as raw edge appliqué and Dresden quilt blocks. In quilting, I've learned there are sometimes many different methods available to achieve the same results. I've shared my preferred methods for each technique as well as three different ways for piecing curves.

HOW TO SEW CURVES

Are you intimidated by sewing curves, but have a list of patterns you'd like to make that include them? Believe me, you're not alone. The not-so-well-known truth about curves is that they're a lot easier to sew than they appear. I have three different methods I teach for sewing curves.

From my own experience and from watching my many students work through the process, I can confidently say that not every method works for everyone. You need to find the method that works for you. Personally, I struggle when I try to sew curves with pins. This surprised me because you'd assume pins holding everything in place would make it easier. I guess my inner, free-spirited self is more confident when I can just wing it with the no-pin method. (What can I say? I've never been great at conforming.) I encourage you to try each method once. Afterward, you will know what works best for you.

Before we begin, I will cover some curve terminology:

- **Convex:** A curve that bends outward. You will see this on the template A piece.

- **Concave:** A curve that bends inward. You will see this on the template B piece.

Curves were a common design element in retro styles and will be used throughout this book.

- **Right Sides Together (RST):** This is when the two "pretty" sides, or fronts, of the fabrics are touching. You're seeing the "ugly" or back side of the fabric.

- **Grain:** The direction of the fiber weaves in fabric. The lengthwise grain runs up and down, parallel to the selvage. This is referred to as **warp**. The cross grain runs left to right, or from selvage to selvage. This is called the **weft**. The weft is made from threads woven over and under the warp threads.

- **Bias:** When you cut the warp and weft at a 45-degree angle, you create a bias grain. The great thing about bias is that it allows fabric to naturally drape around curves and to easily bend. Be cautious with bias because it can easily get stretched out of shape and become warped or misshapen.

- **Drunkard's Path block:** This is a name for a block with a quarter-circle curve in it. In the three methods shown, I will be making a Drunkard's Path block.

PINNING METHOD

Beginning quilters generally tackle curves by using the pinning method. You will also find that most patterns that include curves are written using this method. You can use as many or as few pins as you'd like when sewing curves with pins. The important thing to keep in mind is to remove the pins as you sew. Sewing over the pins can result in breaking the needle and bending the pins.

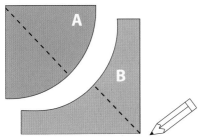

1. Mark the center of both pattern piece A and pattern piece B. You can do this with a marking pen or by folding the piece in half and creating a crease with your finger.

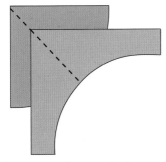

2. Pin both pieces together at their marked centers, RST, with pattern piece A (convex curve) on the bottom and pattern piece B (concave curve) on top.

3. Lining up the raw edges of pattern piece B to pattern piece A, pin the ends together. Be sure not to stretch pattern piece B to fit. Ease the raw edges of both pattern pieces to line up in the spaces between the pins and pin them together as many times as desired.

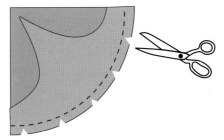

4. Using a ¼" (6.4mm) foot, take your time and slowly sew along the now-convex curve. Be sure to stop between each pin to remove them as you work. Using scissors, snip into the seam allowance, being careful not to cut into the stitching. Snip into the seam about every 1" (2.5cm). This allows the curve to open and lay flat once the block is pressed.

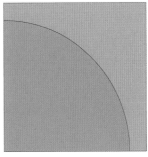

5. Press the block toward the template B piece. Be sure you're pressing and not ironing the block. Due to the bias edges in the block, pushing the iron around will stretch out and warp the block.

NO-PIN METHOD

This is my preferred curves sewing method, but it is the most intimidating to quilters who are new to curves. For this method you won't mark or pin anything.

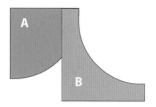

1. Place pieces, RST, with pattern piece B (concave curve) on top and pattern piece A (convex curve) on the bottom. To help me remember the directionality of the pieces, I think of pattern piece A being in the direction of a D and pattern piece B being in the direction of an L.

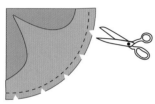

2. Using a ¼" (6.4mm) sewing foot, sew the pieces together along their concave- and convex-curved edge. I work about 1" (2.5cm) at a time, slowly easing the concave edge to line up with the convex edge. Using scissors, snip into the seam allowance, being careful not to cut into the stitching. Snip into the seam about every 1" (2.5cm). This allows the curve to open and lay flat once the block is pressed.

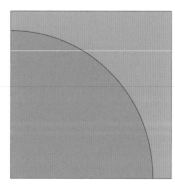

3. Press the block toward the template B piece. Be sure you're pressing and not ironing the block. Due to the bias edges in the block, pushing the iron around will stretch out and warp the block.

GLUE PEN METHOD

This method is the most controversial one for sewing curves. You will either consider it an absolute game changer or will not even consider trying it. This has always been my experience when teaching curves. What surprises quilters the most about this method is that you don't have to go back and remove the glue. Since we're using washable glue, it will wash out. The basic steps for this method are the same as the pinning method.

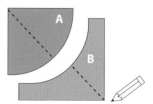

1. Mark the center of both pattern piece A and pattern piece B. You can do this with a marking pen or by folding the piece in half and creating a crease with your finger.

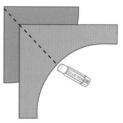

2. Line up both pieces together at their marked centers, RST, with pattern piece A (convex curve) on the bottom and pattern piece B (concave curve) on top. Apply glue to the convex curve at the center. Only apply a thin line of glue.

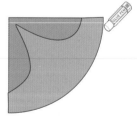

3. Lining up the raw edges of pattern piece B to pattern piece A, slowly apply a thin line of glue to the convex curve. Be sure not to stretch pattern piece B to fit. Ease the raw edges of both pattern pieces to line up all the way around the edge. Using the point of the iron, heat-set the glue. This will prevent the glue from gunking up the needle.

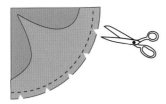

4. Using a ¼" (6.4mm) foot, take your time and slowly sew along the now-convex curve. Using scissors, snip into the seam allowance, being careful not to cut into the stitching. Snip into the seam about every 1" (2.5cm). This allows the curve to open and lay flat once the block is pressed.

5. Press the block toward the template B piece. Be sure you're pressing and not ironing the block. Due to the bias edges in the block, pushing the iron around will stretch out and warp the block.

SQUARING-UP CURVED BLOCKS

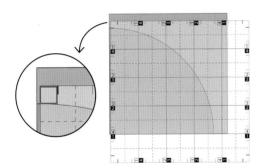

1. After pressing the blocks, they need to be squared up. Line up the ruler's ¼" (6.4mm) mark with the block's seam. Trim.

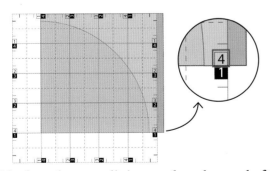

2. Slide the ruler over, lining up the other end of the ruler's ¼" (6.4mm) mark over the block's seam. Trim to the pattern's noted size.

RAW EDGE APPLIQUÉ

Raw edge appliqué is a fun, easy, and modern method for adding imagery with fabric to your quilts. This technique is used throughout the book to apply smaller, detailed elements to the quilts. When using the appliqué templates inside this book, you don't need to add a seam allowance to the templates—this is because we're using the raw edge technique.

1. Trace the appliqué template onto paper or the nonshiny side of the fusible. Cut out the traced appliqué shape at least ¼" (6.4mm) larger than the tracing.

2. Following the instructions that come with your fusible, apply the fusible to the back of the fabric on the fusible's shiny side.

3. Once the fusible has adhered to the fabric, cut the piece out along the drawn line. Place the piece onto the quilt top where you intend to apply it. Heat-set it in place, following the instructions that come with your fusible.

4. Topstitch using either a zigzag, blanket, or satin stitch along the raw edge of the fused piece. I don't recommend using a straight stitch because this can result in issues when it comes to quilting.

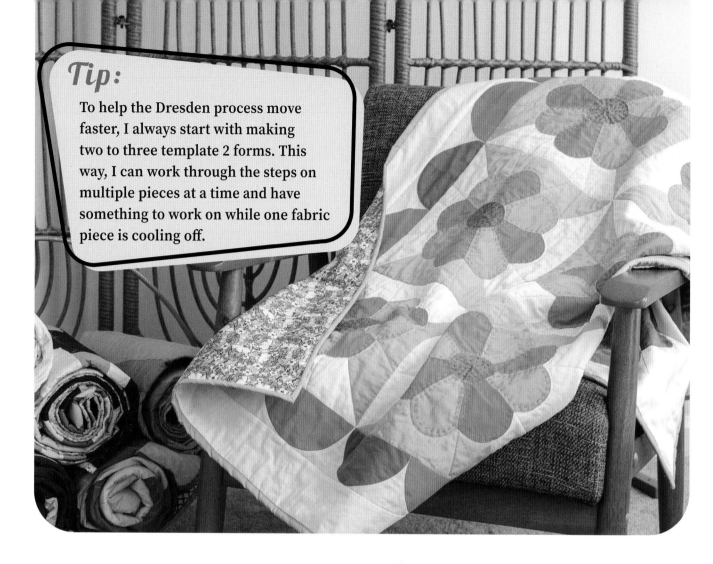

Tip:

To help the Dresden process move faster, I always start with making two to three template 2 forms. This way, I can work through the steps on multiple pieces at a time and have something to work on while one fabric piece is cooling off.

DAISY DRESDEN QUILT BLOCK

Lately I've noticed the traditional Dresden quilt block appearing in modern quilt designs. I love how the block looks effortlessly beautiful in scrappy fabrics as well as in two-color, alternating patterns. What I haven't seen is quilters making the Daisy Dresden quilt block. I think the curved edge at the exterior can seem intimidating to achieve, but it's actually very easy.

The key to a successful Dresden block is accurate cutting and piecing. Being off by ⅛" (3.2mm) will offset all your piecing. Take your time cutting out the pieces and your seam ripper will thank you in the end.

TOOLS & MATERIALS

Starch

Iron

Freezer paper

Tracing tool

Darling Daisies Petal and Appliqué Circle Templates (page 141)

Fusible (I used HeatnBond Iron-On Adhesive)

PETALS

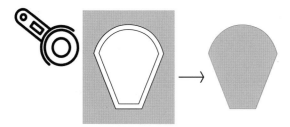

1. Cut the fabric using Petal Fabric Template. If you're having a hard time maneuvering the rotary cutter around the curves, I'd recommend using a smaller 28mm rotary. You can also trace the template onto the fabric and cut the pieces out with fabric scissors.

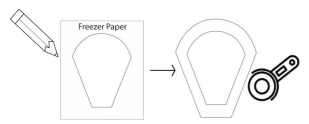

2. Trace Petal Freezer Paper Template onto a piece of freezer paper. Be sure to trace on the rougher, paper-like side and not the shiny side. Cut out the freezer paper roughly 1" (2.5cm) larger than the traced shape.

3. Trim two more pieces of freezer paper to roughly the same size as the first piece. You do not trace the template onto these pieces. Layer the three pieces of freezer paper together with the traced-template piece on top. The rough, paper-like side is facing up and the shiny side is facing down.

4. Press the pieces with the iron until the three layers fuse together as one. Cut out the traced Petal Freezer Paper Template from the fused freezer paper.

5. Place the cut-out fabric piece right side down. Place the fused freezer paper piece shiny side down. Line up the bottoms of the cut-out fabric piece and the Petal Freezer Paper Template. There is a ¼" (6.4mm) gap at the top.

6. Spray starch onto the exposed fabric at the top. If you don't have a spray starch, you can pour some into a small bowl and use a paintbrush to apply the starch. A little will go a long way.

7. Starting from one end, slowly press down the fabric top of the Petal Fabric piece. Move the iron slowly along this edge, pressing the entire seam down. Give the fabric a moment to cool, then peel it off from the fused Petal Freezer Paper Template piece.

8. Repeat steps 1–7 for all the petals. You might find that you need to remake the Petal Freezer Paper Template piece. When peeling the petal piece from it, check that the template hasn't folded over on any of its edges. After a while, it will also lose its ability to stick.

FLOWER

9. After you've pressed all the petals, piece them together in sets of two. Place the same color on top for each pair you're sewing together; not doing so will result in losing the alternating-color pattern.

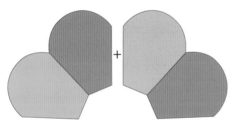

10. Press the seam open. Join two sewn pairs together. Continue with all the petal pairs. Again, make sure you're placing the same color on top each time. Starch the whole piece and press the seam open.

11. Place two sewn units RST, and sew the two edges together as shown. Starch the whole piece and press the seam open.

BACKGROUND

You might notice that the center of the block has a raw edge and may or may not be lining up. Don't worry, we will be covering it up. However, before we add the center of the block, we have to appliqué our Dresden petals onto our background square.

12. Fold the background block in half both ways, creating creases in the center of the block. This can be done from corner to corner; or from top to bottom, and from side to side. The creases are represented by the pink and white colors. Placing the sewn petals right side up on the background block, line the seams of the block up with the creases.

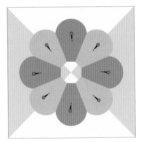

13. Pin the petals in place. I typically only use one pin per petal. Appliqué the petals in place. Since there are clean-folded edges, you could use a blind stitch and hand sew them into place. My preferred method is to use a blanket stitch on my machine to appliqué petals onto the block. If your machine only has a straight stitch option, you can use that as well.

14. From the front of the block going through the hole in the center of the petals, snip a hole into the background square of the block. Turn the block over. Using fabric scissors, slowly cut out the background of the block that is underneath the petals. This reduces bulk and helps the block to lay flatter.

FLOWER CENTER

You're nearly done with the Daisy Dresden block. Now you get to add the center of the flower to the block. There are multiple ways to achieve this. I chose to use raw edge appliqué for my centers. I made this decision because the circle centers can be very difficult to create clean and crisp edges.

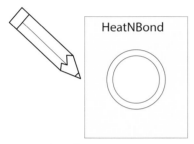

15. Trace the Appliqué Circle template onto the paper side of HeatnBond.

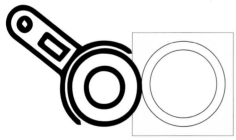

16. Trim the HeatnBond to about ¼" (6.4mm) larger than the traced template as shown. Both a rotary cutter and scissors can be used to cut.

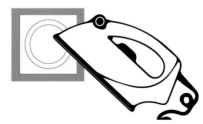

17. Trim the fabric to roughly ¼" (6.4mm) larger than the cut-out HeatnBond piece. Place the shiny side of the HeatnBond on the wrong side of the fabric. Press according to the instructions for your fusible.

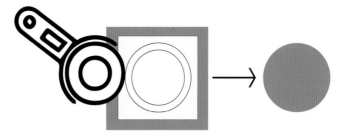

18. Cut out the Appliqué Circle template along the traced lines. Wait to remove the paper until you're ready to apply that piece to the block. Fold the center piece in half both ways, creating a crease at the outside edges. When you're ready to apply the center piece, peel off the paper of the HeatnBond.

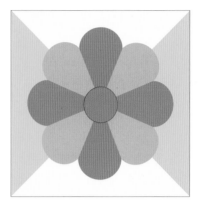

19. Place the Appliqué Circle template piece right side up in the center of the block, lining the creases up with the seams.

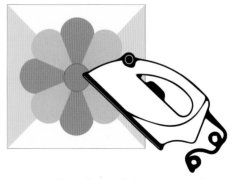

20. Press along the edges of the center piece. If you press in the center of the block, you're likely to get the block stuck to the ironing board. Use your chosen appliqué method to stitch the raw edges down (see step 4 of Raw Edge Appliqué, page 11). I prefer to use the blanket stitch here as well.

BIG STITCH QUILTING

If I had all the time in the world, I would big stitch quilt 100% of all my projects. I love the warm and cozy feeling of snuggling underneath a quilt as I'm pulling bright, thick thread through it. It's the perfect combination of relaxing while still being productive. The other wonderful thing about hand quilting is that you can take it with you. There are quilts in this book that traveled with me on airplanes, hotel rooms, long car rides, and kids' soccer practices. When I look at the stitching in those quilts, I'm transported back to those fond memories.

Unfortunately, I don't have the time to completely hand quilt each project I make. The wonderful thing about big stitch quilting is that it makes for a wonderful accent quilting too. Whenever possible, I'm adding details of big stitch quilting to my quilts. It's my favorite way to add texture, highlight motifs within the quilt design, and incorporate bursts of color.

TOOLS & MATERIALS

8- or 12wt thread

Embroidery needle (any length)

Thimble(s)

Scissors

Marking tool

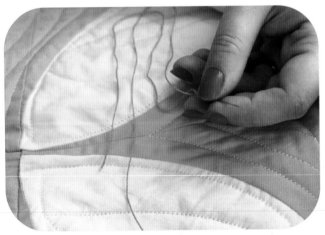

1. Using a removable marking pen or hera marker, plan out your stitching design on the basted quilt top. Thread the needle, leaving one thread tail 2"–3" (5.1–7.6cm) longer than the other. Tie a knot on the longer tail end. If you're using a 12wt thread, you may need 2–3 knots.

Tips:

- **Your thread should never be longer than twice the length of your forearm. This will avoid tangling and knots.**

- **If the needle leaves holes in the fabric where you start and end your stitching, gently scratch the fabric surface, which moves the fabric fibers back into place.**

- **Try using a contrasting thread color to add even more texture and depth to the quilt top. Contrasting thread is also a great way to make a section of the quilt stand out.**

2. Insert the needle into only the top layer of the quilt, sandwiched about ½" (1.3cm) away from where you want to begin stitching. Push the needle out through the top layer where you want to begin stitching.

3. Pull the thread all the way through. With your free hand, apply gentle pressure behind the knot but not on it. Tug the thread, pulling the knot through where the needle entered. The knot will now be sandwiched between the quilt top and the batting where you want to begin the stitching.

4. Begin stitching along the marked design. As you work through the quilt sandwich, only ⅛" (3.2mm) of the sewing needle should extend out of the back. With your working hand, use a rocking motion with the needle, threading it up and down through all the quilt layers. Collect 2–3 stitches onto the needle at a time. Taking multiple stitches at a time helps to keep the stitches balanced and consistent.

Tip:

Do not grip the needle; instead, move it with only one finger. Most people will use either their middle finger or their thumb. Pinching the needle might make you feel like you have better control over the needle, but this is what causes uneven, crooked stitches.

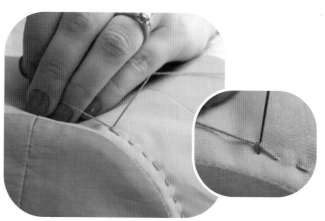

5. Once you have 3"–4" (7.6–10.2cm) remaining of the working thread, remove it from the needle eye. Place the empty needle where you want to end the stitch, going through all the quilt layers. Loosely knot the thread around the needle. Do not make this knot too tight. Remove the needle from both the quilt and knot. This ensures that the knot ends exactly where you want. Rethread the needle. Make the next stitch through only the top layer of the quilt, then push the needle back up through the quilt top about ½" (1.2cm) away from the last stitch.

6. With your free hand, apply gentle pressure behind the knot but not on it. Tug the thread, pulling the knot through to be sandwiched between the quilt top and batting layer. Trim away any remaining thread.

7. Repeat these steps as many times as necessary to complete the marked quilting design.

PROJECTS

Each of the projects inside this book tells a story about the past. While working on these quilts, I found myself becoming nostalgic and remembering fond times with my family and evolving into an adult. My wish is that you, too, are reminded of those wonderful times in your life when you loved the present and were hopeful for the future. I envision each of these quilts being gifted to friends and family members who will also find joy and happy memories within the designs. Spread the love, and I hope you enjoy every stitch.

Rainbow Snails Quilt, 20

Peace, Love & Patchwork Quilt, 26

B-Side Quilt, 34

Darling Daisies Quilt, 42

Double Rainbow Quilt, 48

Marvelous Mushrooms Quilt, 54

Positively Pyrex Quilt, 68

Retro Blooms Quilt, 76

Strawberry Fields Quilt, 82

So Mod Quilt, 94

Retro Stars Quilt, 100

Setting Sun Wall Hanging, 108

Sprout Wall Hanging, 112

Mini Bloom Pillow, 118

Citrus Pillow , 124

Finished size: 62½" x 67" (1.6 x 1.7m)

Skill Level: Intermediate

Fabrics Used: Art Gallery Fabrics in Weathered Brick, Turmeric, Burnt Orange, Cozumel Blue, Coffee Bean, and White Linen

Pieced by Erin Grogan and Kelly Stauffer

Longarmed by Mickie Gelling of Wander Stitch Company

RAINBOW SNAILS QUILT

The rainbow is a timeless motif in design. For me, it represents happiness and playfulness. In the 1960s, we saw the use of the rainbow in psychedelic designs and as a representation of peace and joy. Today, we think of the rainbow as the beauty after a storm. The rainbow is also used as a symbol of inclusion. I wanted a rainbow design that would be great for an adult or for a baby gift. What would be more adorable and perfect than rainbow-shelled snails? They're fun, on a mission, and ready to spark joy.

MATERIALS

Yardage is based on 42" (1.1m) wide fabric. Backing assumes at least 4" (10.2cm) coverage on all sides.

Rainbow Snails Templates (Pages 130–131)

1 yard (91.4cm) in Fabric A (Red)

¾ yard (68.6cm) in Fabric B (Orange)

½ yard (45.7cm) in Fabric C (Yellow)

¼ yard (22.9cm) in Fabric D (Blue)

½ yard (45.7cm) in Fabric E (Brown)

3½ yards (3.2m) in Background (White)

4 yards (3.7m) in backing fabric

½ yard (45.7cm) in binding fabric

71" x 75" (1.8 x 1.9m) in batting

CUTTING

All templates include a ¼" (6.4mm) seam allowance. Mirror image of a template means to turn the template upside down so that the template text is right side touching the fabric.

FROM FABRIC A (RED), CUT:

(8) Template Two

(8) Template Two mirror images

FROM FABRIC B (ORANGE), CUT:

(8) Template Three

(8) Template Three mirror images

FROM FABRIC C (YELLOW), CUT:

(8) Template Four

(8) Template Four mirror images

FROM FABRIC D (BLUE), CUT:

(8) Template Five

(8) Template Five mirror images

FROM FABRIC E (BROWN), CUT:

(4) 3" (7.6cm) x WOF strips, subcut:
    (8) 3" x 5½" (7.6 x 14cm) rectangles
    (8) 3" x 11" (7.6 x 28cm) rectangles
    (16) 1" x 3" (2.5 x 7.6cm) rectangles

FROM BACKGROUND (WHITE), CUT:

(8) Template One

(8) Template One mirror images

(2) 17¼" (43.8cm) x WOF strips, subcut:
    (4) 14" x 17¼" (35.6 x 43.8cm) rectangles
    (4) 8" x 17¼" (20.3 x 43.8cm) rectangles

(10) 2½" (6.4cm) x WOF strips, subcut:
    (16) 2½" x 19½" (6.4 x 49.5cm) strips
    (4) 2½" x 17¼" (6.4 x 43.8cm) strips

(1) 2½" (6.4cm) x WOF strip, subcut:
    (8) 2½" x 3" (6.4 x 7.6cm) rectangles

(8) 2" x 2" (5.1 x 5.1cm) squares

PIECING BLOCK 1

1. Align the top edges of Template Five and Template Four, RST. Template Four should be on top. Stitching slowly, move the raw concave edge of Template Four to line up with the raw edge of Template Five. Use the curve method of your choice (pages 9–10). Snip into the seam, without cutting the stitching, about every ½" (1.2cm). Press the seam open.

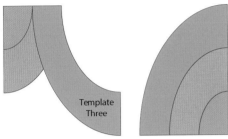

2. Align the top edges of the completed segment and Template Three, RST. Template Three should be on top. Stitching slowly, move the raw concave edge of Template Three to line up with the raw edge of the completed segment. Snip into the seam, without cutting the stitching, about every 1" (2.5cm). Press the seam open.

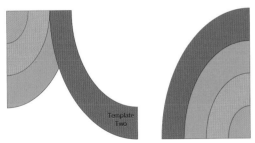

3. Align the top edges of the completed segment and Template Two, RST. Template Two should be on top. Stitching slowly, move the raw concave edge of Template Two to line up with the raw edge of the completed segment. Snip into the seam, without cutting the stitching, about every 1" (2.5cm). Press the seam open.

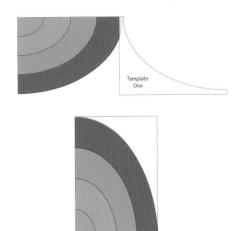

4. Align the top edges of the completed segment and Template One, RST. Template One should be on top. Stitching slowly, move the raw concave edge of Template One to line up with the raw edge of the completed segment. Press the seam open. This makes Block 1.

5. Repeat steps 1–4 to make a total of (8) Block 1s.

PIECING BLOCK 2

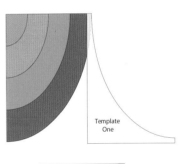

6. Using the mirror-image templates, repeat steps 1–4. This makes the right half of Block 2. Set aside.

7. Mark a diagonal line on the back of a 3" x 5½" (7.6 x 14cm) Fabric E rectangle.

8. Fold the bottom, bottom-right corner to the top left, along the marked line. Press with an iron. Rotate the piece so the bottom edge is horizontal.

9. Align the bottom and left edges of the folded Fabric E rectangle with the bottom-left corner of Block 2. Open the piece so that the fabrics are RST. Pin in place and sew down the marked line. Trim ¼" (6.4mm) away from the sewn line. Press the Fabric E piece toward the bottom-left corner of the block. Set aside.

10. Mark a diagonal line on the back of a 2" x 2" (5.1 x 5.1cm) Background square.

11. Place the marked Background square, RST, in the bottom-left corner of the 3" x 11" (7.6 x 28cm) Fabric E strip. Sew down the marked line. Trim ¼" (6.4mm) away from the sewn line. Press the Background piece toward the bottom-left corner. Set aside.

12. Sew a 1" x 3" (2.5 x 7.6cm) Fabric E strip onto both sides of the 2½" x 3" (6.4 x 7.6cm) Background rectangle. Press toward Fabric E.

13. Sew together the units from steps 11 and 12. Press toward Fabric E. This makes the left half of Block 2.

14. Sew together the two halves of Block 2. Press toward Fabric E. This makes Block 2.

15. Repeat steps 6–14 to make a total of (8) Block 2s.

QUILT TOP ASSEMBLY

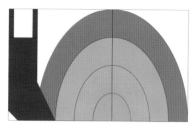

16. Sew Block 2 to the left of Block 1. Press the seam open. Repeat for the remaining units.

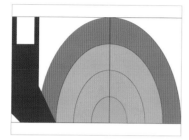

17. Sew a 2½" x 19½" (6.4 x 49.5cm) Background strip to the top and to the bottom of the completed unit. Press toward the Background strips.

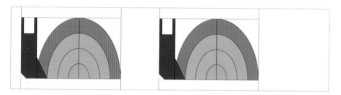

18. Lay out (1) of each Background piece: 2½" x 17¼" (6.4 x 43.8cm) strip, 8" x 17¼" (20.3 x 43.8cm) rectangle, and 14" x 17¼" (35.6 x 43.8cm) rectangle. Refer to the diagram to assemble Row 1. Press the seams toward the Background pieces. Repeat to make Row 3.

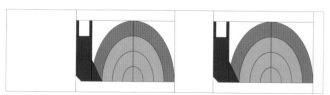

19. Gather (1) of each Background piece: 14" x 17¼" (35.6 x 43.8cm) rectangle, 8" x 17¼" (20.3 x 43.8cm) rectangle, and 2½" x 17¼" (6.4 x 43.8cm) strip. Refer to the diagram to assemble Row 2. Press the seams toward the Background pieces. Repeat to make Row 4.

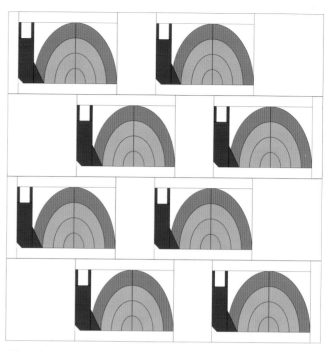

20. Join the (4) rows together as shown to create the quilt top.

FINISHING

21. Make a three-layer quilt sandwich. Make sure the backing piece is at least 2" (5.1cm) larger all the way around the quilt top. Quilt and bind as desired.

Finished Size: 59" x 59" (1.5 x 1.5m)

Skill Level: Intermediate

Fabrics Used: Art Gallery Fabrics Pure Solids Turmeric, Wisteria, Mistic Blue, Creme De La Creme, Patina Green, and Blossomed

Pieced & Quilted
by Erin Grogan

PEACE, LOVE & PATCHWORK QUILT

Peace, Love & Patchwork is inspired by the hippie era that sprouted in the mid-1960s. Hippies were known for their widespread acceptance of religious and cultural diversity, and they embodied a revolutionized vision of the American dream that was deeply rooted in the counterculture of the time. The peace sign is a timeless symbol that represents world peace and is an iconic symbol of the hippies. I chose to include a butterfly within the peace sign because it is a symbol of change and love. These symbols might tell the story of the past, but our desire for change, love, and acceptance is still relevant today.

MATERIALS

Yardage is based on 42" (1.1m) wide fabric. Backing assumes at least 4" (10.2cm) coverage on all sides.

Peace, Love & Patchwork Templates (pages 132–139)

3½ yards (3.2m) in Fabric A (Yellow)

1 yard (91.4cm) in Fabric B (Blue)

½ yard (45.7cm) in Fabric C (Purple)

¼ yard (22.9cm) in Fabric D (White)

¼ yard (22.9cm) in Fabric E (Green)

⅛ yard (11.4cm) in Fabric F (Pink)

4 yards (3.7m) in backing fabric

½ yard (45.7cm) in binding fabric

70" x 70" (1.8 x 1.8m) in batting

CUTTING INSTRUCTIONS

All templates include a ¼" (6.4mm) seam allowance.

FROM FABRIC A (YELLOW), CUT:

(3) Template 3

(3) 16½" x 18" (41.9 x 45.7cm) rectangles

(5) 8½" (21.6cm) x WOF strips, subcut:
- (2) 8½" x 43" (21.6 x 109.2cm) strips
- (2) 8½" x 40½" (21.6 x 102.9cm) strips
- (2) 8½" x 19" (21.6 x 48.3cm) strips

(1) 7¼" x 7¼" (18.4 x 18.4cm) square

(1) 6½" x 14" (16.5 x 35.6cm) strip

(1) 4" x 4" (10.2 x 10.2cm) square

(5) Template 5

(6) Template 7

(1) Template 9

(1) 2½" (6.4cm) x WOF strip, subcut:
- (1) 2½" x 16" (6.4 x 40.6cm) strip
- (3) 2½" x 2½" (6.4 x 6.4cm) squares
- (1) 2½" x 4¾" (6.4 x 12.1cm) rectangle
- (1) 1½" x 2" (3.8 x 5.1cm) rectangle

FROM FABRIC B (BLUE), CUT:

(2) 2½" (6.4cm) x WOF strips, subcut:
- (3) 2½" x 18" (6.4 x 45.7cm) strips
- (1) 2½" x 20" (6.4 x 50.8cm) strip
- (1) 2½" x 24" (6.4 x 61cm) strip
- (1) 2½" x 10⅜" (6.4 x 26.4cm) strip

(3) Template 2

(1) 7¼" x 7¼" (18.4 x 18.4cm) square

(1) Template 8

(2) 1" x 2" (2.5 x 5.1cm) rectangles

FROM FABRIC C (PURPLE), CUT:

(6) Template 4

(6) Template 6

(2) 3½" x 3½" (8.9 x 8.9cm) squares

(8) 1½" x 2" (3.8 x 5.1cm) rectangles

(2) 4½" x 4½" (11.4 x 11.4cm) squares

(8) Appliqué Heart Template

FROM FABRIC D (WHITE), CUT:

(8) 2½" x 2½" (6.4 x 6.4cm) squares

(6) Large Appliqué Flower Template

(10) Small Appliqué Flower Template

(3) Large Appliqué Circle Template

(15) Small Appliqué Circle Template

FROM FABRIC E (GREEN), CUT:

(3) Large Appliqué Flower Template

(15) Small Appliqué Flower Template

(6) Large Appliqué Circle Template

(10) Small Appliqué Circle Template

FROM FABRIC F (PINK), CUT:

(6) Appliqué Heart Template

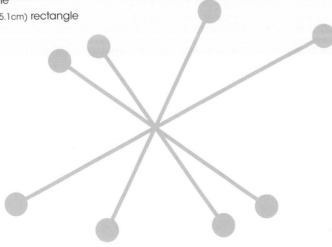

PIECING THE PEACE SIGN

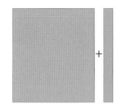

1. Sew a 2½" x 18" (6.4 x 45.7cm) Fabric B strip to the right of a 16½" x 18" (41.9 x 45.7cm) Fabric A piece. Press toward the Fabric B piece.

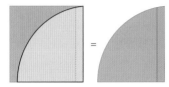

2. Trim the unit with Template 1 as shown.

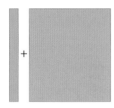

3. Sew a 2½" x 18" (6.4 x 45.7cm) Fabric B strip to the left of a 16½" x 18" (41.9 x 45.7cm) Fabric A piece. Press toward the Fabric B piece.

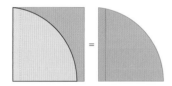

4. Trim the unit with Template 1 as shown.

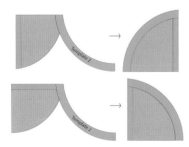

5. Place a Fabric B–Template 2 piece, RST, with the unit from step 2 as shown. Sew the pieces together, gently nesting the Template 2 piece into the curve of the unit. Use the curve method of your choice (pages 9–10). Press toward the Template 2 piece. Repeat with the unit from step 4.

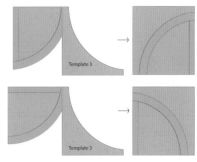

6. Place a Template 3–Fabric A piece, RST, with one unit from step 5 as shown. Sew the pieces together, gently nesting the Template 3 piece into the curve of the unit. Press toward the Template 3 piece. Repeat with the second unit.

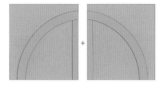

7. Sew the (2) completed units together as shown. Press the seam open.

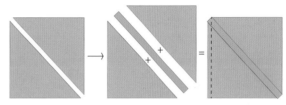

8. Cut a 16½" x 18" (41.9 x 45.7cm) Fabric A piece in half diagonally as shown. Join the two pieces with a 2½" x 24" (6.4 x 61cm) Fabric B strip in the middle. Press toward the Fabric B strip. From the top-left corner, mark a straight line down to the bottom of the unit as shown. Trim along the marked line.

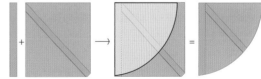

9. Sew a 2½" x 18" (6.4 x 45.7cm) Fabric B strip to the left of the unit. Press toward the Fabric B strip. Trim the unit with Template 1 as shown.

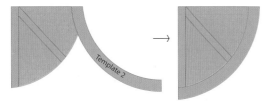

10. Place a Template 2–Fabric B piece, RST, with the unit as shown. Sew the pieces together, gently nesting the Template 2 piece into the curve of the unit. Press toward the Template 2 piece.

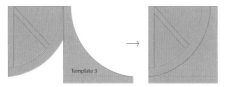

11. Place a Template 3–Fabric A piece, RST, with the unit as shown. Sew the pieces together, gently nesting the Template 3 piece into the curve of the unit. Press toward the Template 3 piece.

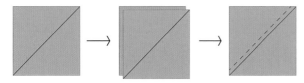

12. Mark a diagonal line on the back of a 7¼" x 7¼" (18.4 x 18.4cm) Fabric B square. Place the marked Fabric B square, RST, with a 7¼" x 7¼" (18.4 x 18.4cm) Fabric A square. Sew ¼" (6.4mm) away from the sewn line.

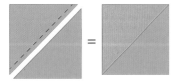

13. Cut along the marked line. Press toward the Fabric B piece. Square the half-square triangle (HST) to 6½" x 6½" (16.5 x 16.5cm).

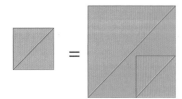

14. Mark a diagonal line on the back of a 4" x 4" (10.2 x 10.2cm) Fabric A square. Place the marked Fabric A square, RST, in the bottom-right corner of the HST. Sew on the marked line.

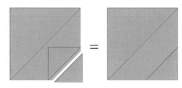

15. Trim ¼" (6.4mm) away from the sewn line. Press toward the Fabric A piece.

PIECING THE BUTTERFLY

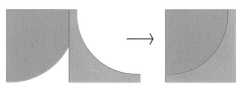

16. Place a Template 5–Fabric A piece, RST, with a Template 4–Fabric C piece as shown. Sew the pieces together, gently nesting the Template 5 piece into the curve of the Template 4 piece. Press toward the Template 5 piece. Square the block to 4½" x 4½" (11.4 x 11.4cm). Make (5) blocks total. Set aside.

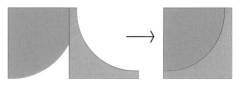

17. Place a Template 7–Fabric A piece, RST, with a Template 6–Fabric C piece as shown. Sew the pieces together, gently nesting the Template 7 piece into the curve of the Template 6 piece. Press toward the Template 7 piece. Square the block to 3½" x 3½" (8.9 x 8.9cm). Make (6) blocks total.

18. Sew a 1½" x 2" (3.8 x 5.1cm) Fabric C piece to the left of a 2½" x 2½" (6.4 x 6.4cm) Fabric D square. Press toward the Fabric C piece. Make (8) units total.

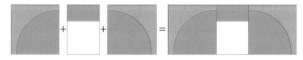

19. Sew a 3½" x 3½" (8.9 x 8.9cm) block from step 17 to both sides of a unit from step 18. Press the seam open. Make (2) units total.

20. Sew a 3½" x 3½" (8.9 x 8.9cm) block from step 17 to the left of a unit from step 17. Sew a 3½" x 3½" (8.9 x 8.9cm) Fabric C square on the right of the unit. Press the seams open. Make (2) units total.

21. Sew a unit from step 18 onto both sides of a 2½" x 2½" (6.4 x 6.4cm) Fabric A square. Press the seam toward the Fabric A piece. Make (2) units total.

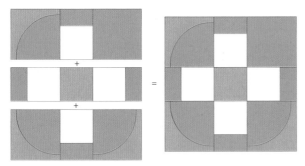

22. Sew the units from steps 19–21 together as shown. Press the seams open. Make (2) blocks total.

23. Sew together Template 8–Fabric B to the Template 9–Fabric A as shown. Press the seam open.

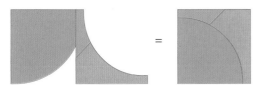

24. Place the unit from step 23, RST, with a Template 4–Fabric C piece as shown. Sew the pieces together, gently nesting the unit piece into the curve of the Template 4 piece. Press toward the unit piece. Square the block to 4½" x 4½" (11.4 x 11.4cm).

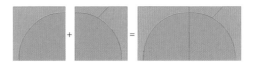

25. Sew a 4½" x 4½" (11.4 x 11.4cm) block from step 16 to the left of the unit as shown. Press the seam open.

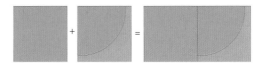

26. Sew a 4½" x 4½" (11.4 x 11.4cm) Fabric C square to the left of a 4½" x 4½" (11.4 x 11.4cm) block from step 16 as shown. Press toward the Fabric C square.

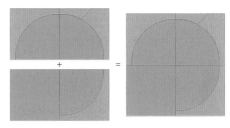

27. Sew the (2) units together, pressing the seam open. This makes the top-right wing of the butterfly. Press the seam open.

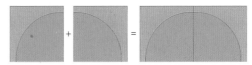

28. Sew together (2) 4½" x 4½" (11.4 x 11.4cm) blocks from step 16 as shown. Press the seam open.

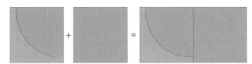

29. Sew a 4½" x 4½" (11.4 x 11.4cm) Fabric C square to the right of a 4½" x 4½" (11.4 x 11.4cm) block from step 16 as shown. Press toward the Fabric C square.

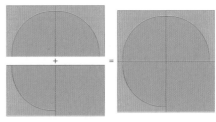

30. Sew the (2) units together, pressing the seam open. This makes the top-left butterfly wing.

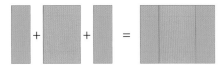

31. Sew a 1" x 2" (2.5 x 5.1cm) Fabric B piece onto both sides of a 1½" x 2" (3.8 x 5.1cm) Fabric A piece. Press toward the Fabric A piece.

32. Sew the unit to the left of a 2½" x 10⅜" (6.4 x 26.4cm) Fabric B strip. Sew a 2½" x 4¾" (6.4 x 12.1cm) Fabric A strip to the right of the Fabric B strip. Press both seams toward the Fabric B strip.

QUILT TOP ASSEMBLY

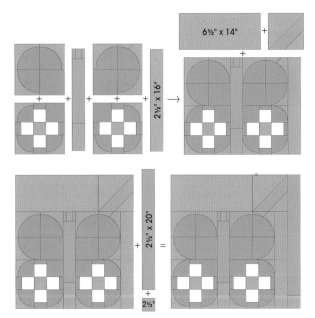

33. Gather the units made in steps 15–32, (1) 2½" x 16" (6.4 x 40.6cm) Fabric A strip, (1) 6½" x 14" (16.5 x 35cm) Fabric A strip, (1) 2½" x 2½" (6.4 x 6.4cm) Fabric A square, and (1) 2½" x 20" (6.4 x 50.8cm) Fabric B strip. Use the diagram to assemble the butterfly.

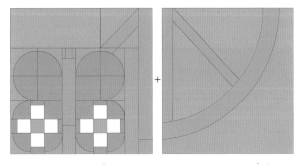

34. Sew the unit from step 11 to the right of the butterfly block. Press the seam open.

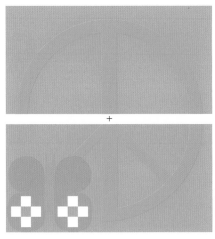

35. Sew the unit from step 7 to the top of the unit. Press the seam open.

36. Sew the 8½" x 43" (21.6 x 109.2cm) Fabric A strips to the sides of the quilt top. Press toward the Fabric A strips.

37. Sew (1) 8½" x 40½" (21.6 x 102.9cm) Fabric A strip to (1) 8½" x 19" (21.6 x 48.3cm) Fabric A strip, creating a 8½" x 59" (21.6 x 149.9cm) strip. Press the seam open. Make two strips total. Sew one strip to the top and one strip to the bottom of the quilt top. Press toward the Fabric A strips.

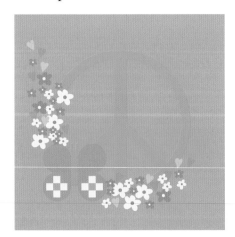

38. Using raw edge appliqué (page 11), apply the small flowers, large flowers, and heart appliqué pieces to the quilt top as desired. You can layer and overlap the pieces.

FINISHING

39. Make a three-layer quilt sandwich. Make sure the backing piece is at least 2" (5.1cm) larger all the way around the quilt top. Quilt and bind as desired.

Finished Size: 60" x 60" (1.5 x 1.5m)

Skill Level: Intermediate

Fabrics Used: Art Gallery
Fabrics Pure Solids Desert Dunes,
Turmeric, Wisteria, Cozemel Blue,
Sweet Tangerine, Blossomed,
Patina Green, and White Linen

Pieced by Kelly Stauffer

Quilted by Mickie Gelling

B-SIDE QUILT

When you recall the music of the 1960s and 1970s, you immediately think of the "British Invasion" from artists like The Beatles and The Rolling Stones. This was also a thriving era for soul and R & B music from artists like Aretha Franklin and Diana Ross. B-Side is a nod to all the musical stars that played on constant repeat in every household and dance hall.

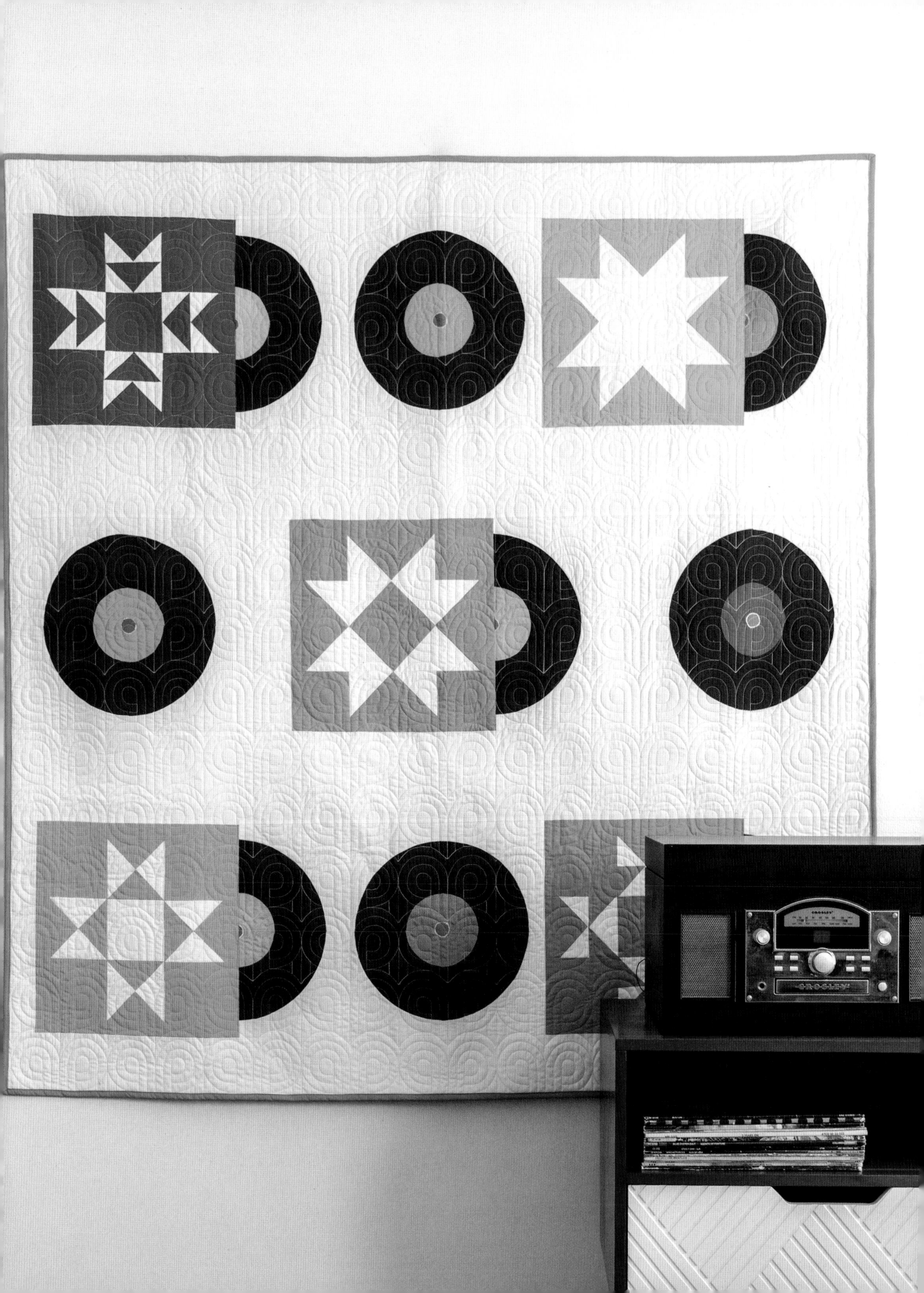
CROSLEY

MATERIALS

Yardage is based on 42" (1.1m) wide fabric.

B-Side Templates (page 140)

⅓ yard (30.5cm) in Fabric A (Red)

¼ yard (22.9cm) in Fabric B (Yellow)

⅓ yard (30.5cm) in Fabric C (Purple)

¼ yard (22.9cm) in Fabric D (Orange)

⅓ yard (30.5cm) in Fabric E (Teal)

⅛ yard (11.4cm) in Fabric F (Pink)

⅛ yard (11.4cm) in Fabric G (Green)

1 yard (91.4cm) in Fabric H (Charcoal)

⅛ yard (11.4cm) in Fabric I (Light Gray)

2½ yards (2.3m) in Background (White)

4 yards (3.7m) in backing fabric

½ yard (45.7cm) in binding fabric

70" x 70" (1.8 x 1.8m) in batting

CUTTING

All templates include a ¼" (6.4mm) seam allowance.

FROM FABRIC A (RED), CUT:

(4) 5½" x 5½" (14 x 14cm) squares

(1) 4½" (11.4cm) x WOF strip, subcut:
- (1) 4½" x 4½" (11.4 x 11.4cm) square
- (4) 4½" x 3½" (11.4 x 8.9cm) rectangles
- (4) 4½" x 2½" (11.4 x 6.4cm) rectangles
- (4) Template 1

FROM FABRIC B (YELLOW), CUT:

(1) 6½" (16.5cm) x WOF strip, subcut:
- (4) 6½" x 4½" (16.5 x 11.4cm) rectangles
- (4) 4½" x 4½" (11.4 x 11.4cm) squares
- (2) Template 1

FROM FABRIC C (PURPLE), CUT:

(1) 6½" (16.5cm) x WOF strip, subcut:
- (1) 6½" x 6½" (16.5 x 16.5cm) square
- (4) 6½" x 4½" (16.5 x 11.4cm) rectangles
- (2) Template 1

(4) 4½" x 4½" (11.4 x 11.4cm) squares

FROM FABRIC D (ORANGE), CUT:

(6) 5½" x 5½" (14 x 14cm) squares

(4) 1½" x 4½" (3.8 x 11.4cm) strips

(4) Template 1

FROM FABRIC E (TEAL), CUT:

(1) 5½" (14cm) x WOF strip, subcut:
- (4) 5½" x 5½" (14 x 14cm) squares
- (4) Template 1

(1) 4½" (11.4cm) x WOF strip, subcut:
- (1) 4½" x 4½" (11.4 x 11.4cm) square
- (4) 4½" x 3½" (11.4 x 8.9cm) rectangles
- (8) 2½" x 2½" (6.4 x 6.4cm) squares

FROM FABRIC F (PINK), CUT:

(4) Template 1

FROM FABRIC G (GREEN), CUT:

(6) Template 1

FROM FABRIC H (CHARCOAL), CUT:

(5) 6" (15.2cm) x WOF strips, subcut:
- (26) Template 2

FROM FABRIC I (LIGHT GRAY), CUT:

(9) Circle Center Appliqué pieces

FROM BACKGROUND (WHITE), CUT:

(8) 6½" (16.5cm) x WOF strips, subcut:
- (2) 6½" x 40" (16.5 x 101.6cm) strips
- (2) 6½" x 20½" (16.5 x 52.1cm) strips
- (1) 6½" x 6½" (16.5 x 16.5cm) square
- (26) Template 3

(2) 5½" x 5½" (14 x 14cm) squares

(2) 4½" x 14½" (11.4 x 36.8cm) strips

(1) 4½" x 4½" (11.4 x 11.4cm) square

(5) 3½" (8.9cm) x WOF strips, subcut:
- (2) 3½" x 40" (8.9 x 101.6cm) strips
- (2) 3½" x 20½" (8.9 x 52.1cm) strips
- (20) 3½" x 3½" (8.9 x 8.9cm) squares

(5) 2½" (6.4cm) x WOF strips, subcut:
- (6) 2½" x 14½" (6.4 x 36.8cm) strips
- (4) 2½" x 4½" (6.4 x 10.2cm) xsrectangles
- (24) 2½" x 2½" (6.4 x 6.4cm) squares

PIECING SLEEVE 1

1. Mark a diagonal line on the back of (16) 2½" x 2½" (6.4 x 6.4cm) Background squares as shown.

2. Place a marked Background square, RST, in the top-left corner of a 4½" x 2½" (11.4 x 6.4cm) Fabric A strip as shown. Sew down the marked line. Trim ¼" (6.4mm) away from the sewn line and press toward the Background piece.

3. Place a marked Background square, RST, in the top-right corner of the unit as shown. Sew down the marked line. Trim ¼" (6.4mm) away from the sewn line and press toward the Background piece. Trim the block to 4½" x 2½" (11.4 x 6.4cm). This creates a Flying Geese block. Make (4) blocks total.

4. Place a marked Background square, RST, in the top-left corner of a 4½" x 3½" (11.4 x 8.9cm) Fabric A piece as shown. Sew down the marked line. Trim ¼" (6.4mm) away from the sewn line and press toward the Background piece.

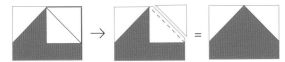

5. Place a marked Background square, RST, in the top-right corner of the unit as shown. Sew down the marked line. Trim ¼" (6.4mm) away from the sewn line and press toward the Background piece. Trim the block to 4½" x 3½" (11.4 x 8.9cm). This completes the Covered-Corner block. Make (4) blocks total.

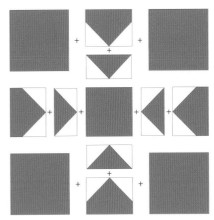

6. Sew together (4) Flying Geese blocks, (4) Covered-Corner blocks, (4) 5½" x 5½" (14 x 14cm) Fabric A squares, and (1) 4½" x 4½" (11.4 x 11.4cm) Fabric A square using the Sleeve 1 Assembly Diagram. Press the seams toward the Fabric A squares. Square the block to 14½" x 14½" (36.8 x 36.8cm).

PIECING SLEEVE 2

7. Mark a diagonal line on the back of (8) 3½" x 3½" (8.9 x 8.9cm) Background squares.

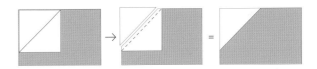

8. Place a marked Background square, RST, in the top-left corner of a 6½" x 4½" (16.5 x 11.4cm) Fabric B piece as shown. Sew down the marked line. Trim ¼" (6.4mm) away from the sewn line and press toward the Background piece. Trim the block to 6½" x 4½" (16.5 x 11.4cm).

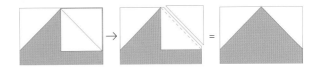

9. Place a marked Background square, RST, in the top-right corner of the unit as shown. Sew down the marked line. Trim ¼" (6.4mm) away from the sewn line and press toward the Background piece. This completes the Covered-Corner block. Make (4) blocks total.

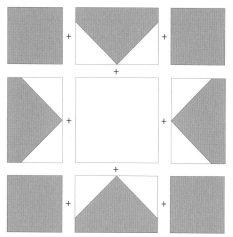

10. Sew together (4) Covered-Corner blocks, (4) 4½" x 4½" (11.4 x 11.4cm) Fabric B squares, and (1) 6½" x 6½" (16.5 x 16.5cm) Background square using the Sleeve 2 Assembly Diagram. Press away from the Covered-Corner blocks. Square the block to 14½" x 14½" (36.8 x 36.8cm).

PIECING SLEEVE 3

11. Mark a diagonal line on the back of (12) 3½" x 3½" (8.9 x 8.9cm) Background squares.

12. Place a marked Background square, RST, in the top-left corner of a 6½" x 4½" (16.5 x 11.4cm) Fabric C piece as shown. Sew down the marked line. Trim ¼" (6.4mm) away from the sewn line and press toward the Background piece. Trim the block to 6½" x 4½" (16.5 x 11.4cm).

13. Place a marked Background square, RST, in the top-right corner of the unit as shown. Sew down the marked line. Trim ¼" (6.4mm) away from the sewn line and press toward the Background piece. This completes the Covered-Corner block. Make (4) blocks total.

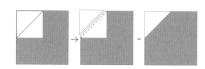

14. Place a marked Background square, RST, in the top-left corner of a 6½" x 6½" (16.5 x 16.5cm) Fabric C square as shown. Sew down the marked line. Trim ¼" (6.4mm) away from the sewn line and press toward the Background piece.

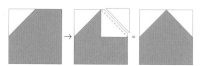

15. Place a marked Background square, RST, in the top-right corner of the unit as shown. Sew down the marked line. Trim ¼" (6.4mm) away from the sewn line and press toward the Background piece.

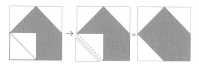

16. Place a marked Background square, RST, in the bottom-left corner of the unit as shown. Sew down the marked line. Trim ¼" (6.4mm) away from the sewn line and press toward the Background piece.

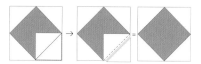

17. Place a marked Background square, RST, in the bottom-right corner of the unit as shown. Sew down the marked line. Trim ¼" (6.4mm) away from the sewn line and press toward the Background piece. Square the block to 6½" x 6½" (16.5 x 16.5cm). This completes the Economy block.

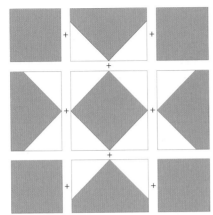

18. Sew together (4) Covered-Corner blocks, (1) Economy block, and (4) 4½" x 4½" (11.4 x 11.4cm) Fabric C squares together using the Sleeve 3 Assembly Diagram. Press the seams open. Square the block to 14½" x 14½" (36.8 x 36.8cm).

PIECING SLEEVE 4

19. Mark a diagonal line on the back of (2) 5½" x 5½" (14 x 14cm) Background squares.

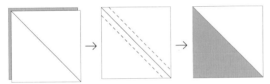

20. Place a marked Background square, RST, with a 5½" x 5½" (14 x 14cm) Fabric D square. Sew ¼" (6.4mm) away on both sides of the marked line. Cut along the marked line and press toward the Fabric D pieces. This will yield (2) HSTs.

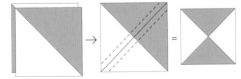

21. Place the (2) HSTs, RST, with alternating fabrics touching as shown. Mark a diagonal line on the back of one of the HST, going in the alternate direction of the previous seam. Sew ¼" (6.4mm) away on both sides of the marked line. Cut along the marked line and press the seam open. Square the block to 4½" x 4½" (11.4 x 11.4cm). This will yield (2) Hourglass blocks. Make (4) blocks total.

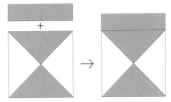

22. Sew a 1½" x 4½" (3.8 x 11.4cm) Fabric D strip to the top of each Hourglass block as shown. Press toward the Fabric D strip.

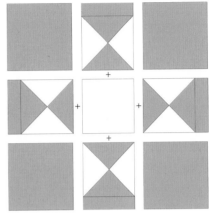

23. Sew together the (4) Hourglass units, (4) 5½" x 5½" (14 x 14cm) Fabric D squares, and (1) 4½" x 4½" (11.4 x 11.4cm) Background square together using the Sleeve 4 Assembly Diagram. Press the seams toward the solid blocks. Square the block to 14½" x 14½" (36.8 x 36.8cm).

PIECING SLEEVE 5

24. Mark a diagonal line on the back of (8) 2½" x 2½" (6.4 x 6.4cm) Background squares and (8) 2½" x 2½" (6.4 x 6.4cm) Fabric E squares as shown.

25. Place a marked Fabric E square, RST, in the top-left corner of a 2½" x 4½" (6.4 x 10.2cm) Background strip as shown. Sew down the marked line. Trim ¼" (6.4mm) away from the sewn line and press toward the Fabric E piece. Trim the block to 2½" x 4½" (6.4 x 10.2cm).

26. Place a marked Fabric E square, RST, in the top-right corner of the unit as shown. Sew down the marked line. Trim ¼" (6.4mm) away from the sewn line and press toward the Fabric E piece. Trim the block to 2½" x 4½" (6.4 x 10.2cm). This creates a Flying Geese block. Make (4) blocks total.

27. Place a marked Background square, RST, in the top-left corner of a 4½" x 3½" (11.4 x 8.9cm) Fabric E piece as shown. Sew down the marked line. Trim ¼" (6.4mm) away from the sewn line and press toward the Background piece.

28. Place a marked Background square, RST, in the top-right corner of the unit as shown. Sew down the marked line. Trim ¼" (6.4mm) away from the sewn line and press toward the Background piece. Trim the block to 4½" x 3½" (11.4 x 8.9cm). This completes the Covered-Corner block. Make (4) blocks total.

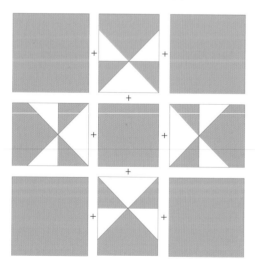

29. Sew together the (4) Flying Geese blocks, (4) Covered-Corner blocks, (4) 5½" x 5½" (14 x 14cm) Fabric E squares, and (1) 4½" x 4½" (11.4 x 11.4cm) Fabric E square using the Sleeve 5 Assembly Diagram. Press the seams toward the Fabric E blocks. Square the block to 14½" x 14½" (36.8 x 36.8cm).

PIECING THE RECORD BLOCK

30. Place a Template 2–Fabric H piece, RST, with a Template 1–color piece as shown. Sew the pieces together, gently nesting the Template 2 piece into the curve of the Template 1 piece. Use the curve method of your choice (pages 9–10). Press toward the Template 2 piece.

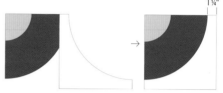

31. Place a Template 3–Background piece, RST, with the unit as shown. Sew the pieces together, gently nesting the Template 3 piece into the curve of the unit. Press toward the Template 3 piece. Square the block to 7½" x 7½" (19.1 x 19.1cm), leaving 1¼" (3.2cm) of Background as shown. This completes the Record block.

32. Repeat steps 30 and 31 to make (26) Record blocks total.

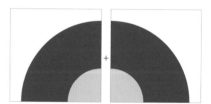

33. Sew together (2) same-color Record blocks as shown. Press the seam open. Trim the unit to 7½" x 14½" (19.1 x 36.8cm). Make (13) units total.

QUILT TOP ASSEMBLY

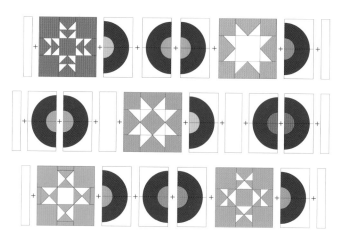

34. Sew together the Sleeve 1–5 blocks, (13) Record units, (6) 2½" x 14½" (6.4 x 36.8cm) Background strips, and (2) 4½" x 14½" (11.4 x 36.8cm) Background strips using the Row Assembly Diagram to assemble Rows 1–3 of the quilt top.

35. Using raw edge appliqué (page 11), apply the Fabric I circles to the center of all the Record units.

36. Sew (1) 6½" x 40" (16.5 x 101.6cm) Background strip to (1) 6½" x 20½" (16.5 x 52.1cm) Background strip together, creating a 6½" x 60" (16.5 x 152.4cm) strip. Press the seam open. Make (2) strips total.

37. Sew (1) 6½" x 60" (16.5 x 152.4cm) Background strip between Rows 1 and 2. Press toward the Background strip. Sew (1) 6½" x 60" (16.5 x 152.4cm) Background strip between Rows 2 and 3. Press toward the Background strip.

38. Sew (1) 3½" x 40" (8.9 x 101.6cm) Background strip to (1) 3½" x 20½" (8.9 x 52.1cm) Background strip, creating a 3½" x 60" (8.9 x 152.4cm) strip. Press the seam open. Make two strips total. Sew one strip to the top and one strip to the bottom of the quilt top. Press toward the Background strips, completing the quilt top.

FINISHING

39. Make a three-layer quilt sandwich. Make sure the backing piece is at least 2" (5.1cm) larger all the way around the quilt top. Quilt and bind as desired.

Finished size: 60" x 60" (1.5 x 1.5m)

Skill Level: Intermediate

Fabrics Used: Art Gallery Pure Solids Creme De La Creme, Burnt Orange, Blossomed, Asparagus, and Marmalade

Pieced & Quilted by Erin Grogan

DARLING DAISIES QUILT

Retro houseware was loud, eclectic, and rather optimistic, and I wanted to channel that style in the Darling Daisies pattern. While working on this quilt, I kept referring to it as Grandmother's Kitchen. It transports me back to time spent together with loved ones gathered around the kitchen table. Family members would be sharing stories of their childhood or the latest news around town while sounds of clanging pots and pans can be heard just over the chatter. Darling Daisies uses a daisy-shaped Dresden Block, which represents everyone coming together at the dinner table.

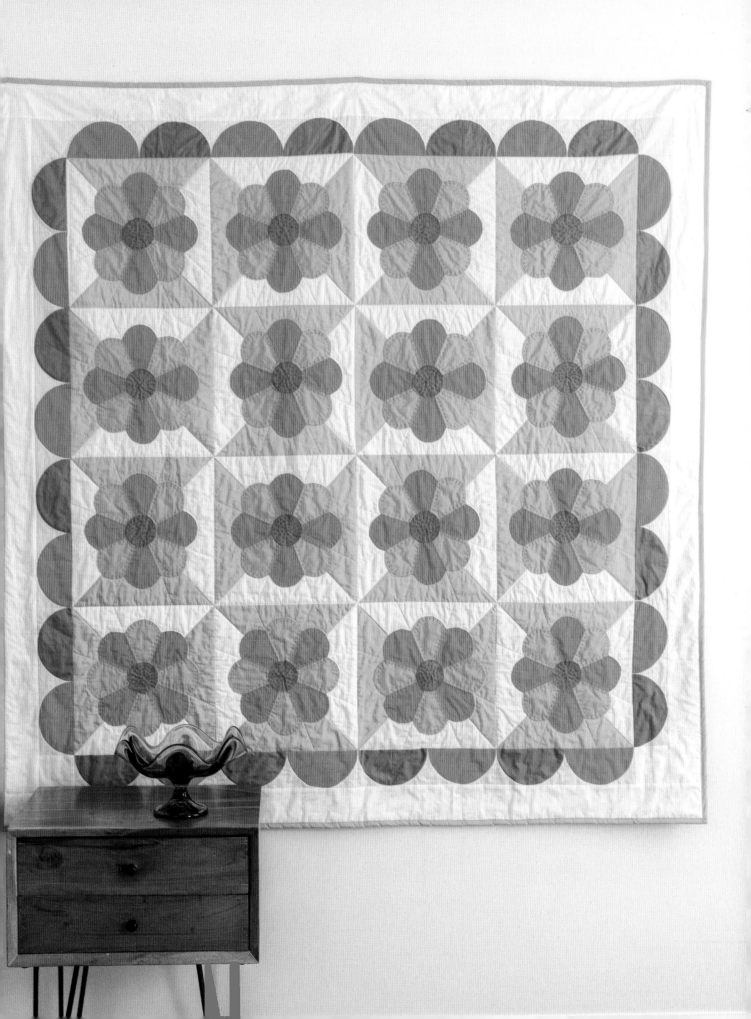

MATERIALS

Yardage is based on 42" (1.1m) wide fabric. Backing assumes at least 4" (10.2cm) coverage on all sides.

Darling Daisies Templates (page 141)

1¼ yards (1.1m) in Fabric A (Pink)

1 yard (91.4cm) in Fabric B (Dark Orange)

½ yard (45.7cm) in Fabric C (Light Orange)

½ yard (45.7cm) in Fabric D (Green)

2½ yards (2.3m) in Background (White)

4 yards (3.7m) in backing fabric

½ yard (45.7cm) in binding fabric

70" x 70" (1.8 x 1.8m) in batting

Daisy Dresden tools & materials (page 12)

CUTTING

All templates include a ¼" (6.4mm) seam allowance.

FROM FABRIC A (PINK), CUT:

(7) 6¼" (15.9cm) x WOF strips, subcut:
   (32) Template 3

FROM FABRIC B (DARK ORANGE), CUT:

(4) 4½" (11.4cm) x WOF strips, subcut:
   (64) Petal Fabric Template

(4) 3¾" (9.5cm) x WOF strips, subcut:
   (32) Template 1

FROM FABRIC C (LIGHT ORANGE), CUT:

(4) 4½" (11.4cm) x WOF strips, subcut:
   (64) Petal Fabric Template

FROM FABRIC D (GREEN), CUT:

(4) 3¾" (9.5cm) x WOF strips, subcut:
   (32) Template 1

(1) 2½" (6.4cm) x WOF strip, subcut:
   (16) Appliqué Center Circles

FROM BACKGROUND (WHITE), CUT:

(7) 6¼" (15.9cm) x WOF strips, subcut:
   (32) Template 3

(4) 4" (10.2cm) x WOF strips, subcut:
   (64) Template 2

(6) 3½" (8.9cm) x WOF strips, subcut:
   (4) 3½" x 40" (8.9 x 101.6cm) strips
   (2) 3½" x 20½" (8.9 x 52.1cm) strips
   (2) 3½" x 13½" (8.9 x 34.3cm) strips
   (4) 3½" x 3½" (8.9 x 8.9cm) squares

FROM FREEZER PAPER, CUT:

(128) Petal Freezer Paper Template

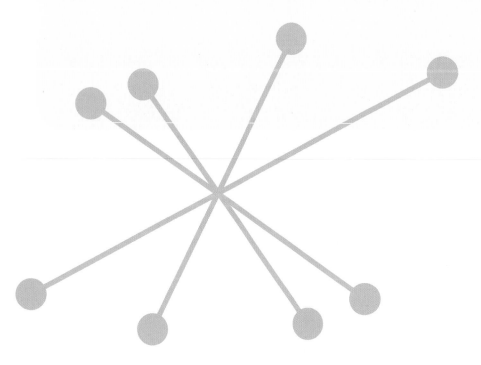

PIECING THE BACKGROUND BLOCK

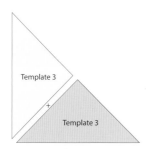

1. Sew a Template 3–Background piece to the left of a Template 3–Fabric A piece on their short edge as shown. Press the seam toward the Fabric A piece. Make (32) units total.

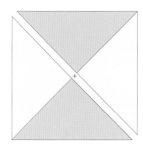

2. Sew together (2) units on their long edge as shown, nesting their center seam. Press the seam open. Square the block to 12" x 12" (30.5 x 30.5cm). This creates a Background block. Make (16) blocks total.

PIECING THE DRESDEN BLOCK

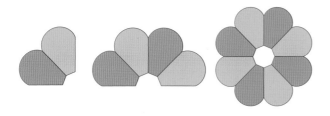

3. Using the Daisy Dresden Quilt Block instructions (pages 12–15), make (64) Fabric B petals and (64) Fabric C petals. Each Dresden block is made with (4) Fabric B and (4) Fabric C petals, alternating. Make (16) Dresden flowers total.

4. Appliqué the Dresden blocks to the Background blocks using the appliqué instructions (page 11).

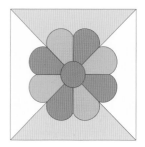

5. Make (16) center circle Fabric D pieces. Appliqué the centers to the Dresden units. This completes the Dresden block for (16) total.

PIECING THE DRUNKARD'S PATH BLOCK

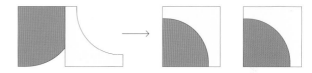

6. Place a Template 2–Background piece, RST, with a Template 1–color piece as shown. Sew the pieces together, gently nesting the Template 2 piece into the curve of the Template 1 piece. Use the curve method of your choice (pages 9–10). Press toward the Template 2 piece. Square the Drunkard's Path block to 3½" x 3½" (8.9 x 8.9cm). Make (32) Fabric B Drunkard's Path blocks and (32) Fabric D Drunkard's Path blocks total.

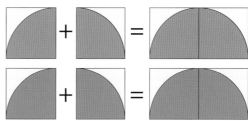

7. Sew together (2) same-color Drunkard's Path blocks as shown. Press the seam open. This creates a half circle. Make (16) Fabric B half circles and (16) Fabric D half circles.

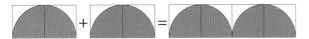

8. Sew a Fabric B half circle to the left of a Fabric D half circle. Press the seam open. Make (16) sets.

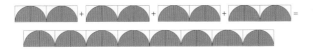

9. Sew (4) sets together as shown, making a strip of (8) alternating half circles. Press the seams open. Make (4) strips total.

QUILT TOP ASSEMBLY

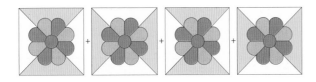

10. Sew (4) completed Dresden blocks together, rotating the direction of the block as shown. Repeat with the remaining blocks to make (4) rows total.

11. Sew the rows together, ensuring that they rotate as shown.

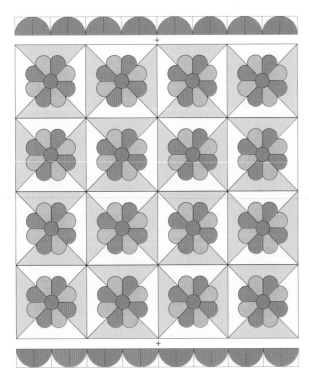

12. Sew a half-circle strip to the top and the bottom of the quilt top. Press the seam open.

13. Sew a 3½" x 3½" (8.9 x 8.9cm) Background square onto both ends of the remaining half-circle strips. Press toward the Background squares.

14. Sew the remaining half-circle strips onto the sides of the quilt top. Press the seam open.

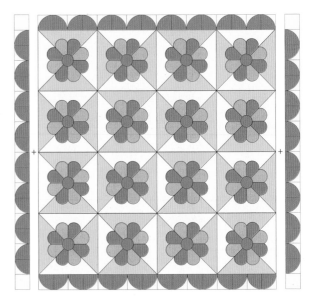

15. Sew (1) 3½" x 40" strips (8.9 x 101.6cm) Background strip to (1) 3½" x 13½" (8.9 x 34.3cm) Background strip. This creates a 3½" x 53" (8.9 x 134.6cm) strip. Make (2) strips total.

16. Sew a 3½" x 53" (8.9 x 134.62cm) Background strip to the top and to the bottom of the quilt top. Press toward the Background strip.

17. Sew (1) 3½" x 40" strips (8.9 x 101.6cm) Background strip to a 3½" x 20½" (8.9 x 52.1cm) Background strip. This creates a 3½" x 60" (8.9 x 152.4cm) strip. Make (2) strips total.

18. Sew the 3½" x 60" (8.9 x 152.4cm) Background strips to the sides of the quilt top. Press toward the Background strips.

FINISHING

19. Make a three-layer quilt sandwich. Make sure the backing piece is at least 2" (5.1cm) larger all the way around the quilt top. Quilt and bind as desired.

Finished Size: 57" x 70" (1.4 x 1.8m)

Skill Level: Intermediate

Fabrics Used: Art Gallery Fabrics Pure Solids Royal Cobalt, Emerald, Canary, Burnt Orange, Aurora Red, and Coconut Milk

Pieced by Kelly Stauffer

Quilted by Erin Grogan

DOUBLE RAINBOW QUILT

If you happen to come across a double rainbow after a storm, it's a sign that good things are to come your way. The 1960s and 1970s were an era of transformation. The double rainbow is seen as a symbol of change and a sign of hope. The era was fueled by optimism for the future with a desire to reflect, meditate, discover, and grow.

MATERIALS

Yardage is based on 42" (1.1m) wide fabric. Backing assumes at least 4" (10.2cm) coverage on all sides.

Double Rainbow Templates (pages 142–144)

⅔ yard (61cm) in Fabric A (Blue)

⅔ yard (61cm) in Fabric B (Green)

⅔ yard (61cm) in Fabric C (Yellow)

⅔ yard (61cm) in Fabric D (Orange)

1 yard (91.4cm) in Fabric E (Red)

2 yards (1.8m) in Background (White)

4 yards (3.7m) in backing fabric

½ yard (45.7cm) in binding fabric

67" x 80" (1.7 x 2m) in batting

CUTTING

All templates include a ¼" (6.4mm) seam allowance.

FROM FABRIC A (BLUE), CUT:

(2) Template 2

(3) 4½" (11.4cm) x WOF strips, subcut:
  (2) 4½" x 30" (11.4 x 76.2cm) strips
  (1) 4½" x 20" (11.4 x 50.8cm) strip
  (1) 4½" x 16" (11.4 x 40.6cm) strip
  (2) 4½" x 4½" (11.4 x 11.4cm) squares
  (2) Template 1

FROM FABRIC B (GREEN), CUT:

(2) Template 2

(3) 4½" (11.4cm) x WOF strips, subcut:
  (1) 4½" x 34" (11.4 x 86.4cm) strip
  (1) 4½" x 30" (11.4 x 76.2cm) strip
  (2) 4½" x 20" (11.4 x 50.8cm) strips
  (4) 4½" x 4½" (11.4 x 11.4cm) squares
  (2) Template 1

FROM FABRIC C (YELLOW), CUT:

(2) Template 2

(4) 4½" (11.4cm) x WOF strips, subcut:
  (1) 4½" x 38" (11.4 x 96.5cm) strip
  (1) 4½" x 30" (11.4 x 76.2cm) strip
  (1) 4½" x 24" (11.4 x 61cm) strip
  (1) 4½" x 20" (11.4 x 50.8cm) strip
  (6) 4½" x 4½" (11.4 x 11.4cm) squares
  (2) Template 1

FROM FABRIC D (ORANGE), CUT:

(2) Template 2

(4) 4½" (11.4cm) x WOF strips, subcut:
  (1) 4½" x 42" (11.4 x 106.7cm) strip
  (1) 4½" x 30" (11.4 x 76.2cm) strip
  (1) 4½" x 28" (11.4 x 71.1cm) strip
  (1) 4½" x 20" (11.4 x 50.8cm) strip
  (8) 4½" x 4½" (11.4 x 11.4cm) squares
  (2) Template 1

FROM FABRIC E (RED), CUT:

(2) Template 2

(5) 4½" (11.4cm) x WOF strips, subcut:
  (1) 4½" x 40" (11.4 x 101.6cm) strip
  (1) 4½" x 32" (11.4 x 81.3cm) strip
  (1) 4½" x 30" (11.4 x 76.2cm) strip
  (1) 4½" x 20" (11.4 x 50.8cm) strip
  (1) 4½" x 6½" (11.4 x 16.5cm) rectangle
  (10) 4½" x 4½" (11.4 x 11.4cm) square
  (2) Template 1

FROM BACKGROUND (WHITE), CUT:

(2) 15" (38.1cm) x WOF strips, subcut:
  (2) Template 3
  (1) Template 4

(1) 5½" (14cm) x WOF strip, subcut:
  (1) 5½" x 15" (14 x 38.1cm) strip
  (2) Template 2

(8) 4½" (11.4cm) x WOF strips, subcut:
  (2) 4½" (11.4cm) x WOF strips
  (1) 4½" x 31" (11.4 x 78.7cm) strip
  (1) 4½" x 27" (11.4 x 68.6cm) strip
  (2) 4½" x 26" (11.4 x 66cm) strips
  (1) 4½" x 23" (11.4 x 58.4cm) strip
  (1) 4½" x 19" (11.4 x 48.3cm) strip
  (1) 4½" x 18" (11.4 x 45.7cm) strip
  (1) 4½" x 12" (11.4 x 30.5cm) strip
  (2) Template 1

PIECING THE DRUNKARD'S PATH BLOCK

DRUNKARD'S PATH CHART

		Template 1	Template 2
A	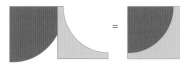	Background	Fabric A
B		Fabric A	Fabric B
C		Fabric B	Fabric C
D		Fabric C	Fabric D
E		Fabric D	Fabric E
F		Fabric E	Background

1. Place a Template 2 piece, RST, with a Template 1 piece as shown. Sew the pieces together, gently nesting the Template 2 piece into the curve of the Template 1 piece. Use the curve method of your choice (pages 9–10). Press toward the Template 2 piece. Square the Drunkard's Path block to 4½" x 4½" (11.4 x 11.4cm). Make (12) Drunkard's Path blocks total using the chart for reference.

PIECING SECTION 1

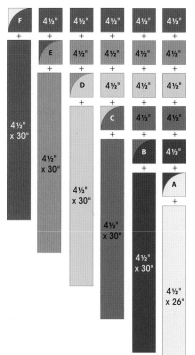

2. Sew together the (6) individual columns as shown. Press the seam open.

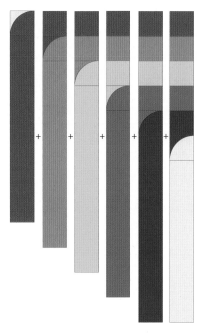

3. Sew the columns together, lining them up at the top of the 4½" x 4½" (11.4 x 11.4cm) Fabric E squares. Press the seams open.

PIECING SECTION 2

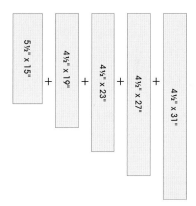

4. Sew together the (5) Background strips as shown. Press the seams open.

PIECING SECTION 3

5. Sew together the 4½" x 6½" (11.4 x 16.5cm) Fabric E rectangle to the 4½" x 40" (11.4 x 101.6cm) Fabric E strip. This will create a 4½" x 46" (11.4 x 116.8cm) Fabric E strip.

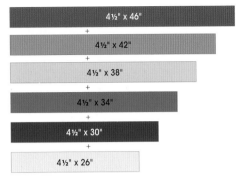

6. Beginning with the 4½" x 46" (11.4 x 116.8cm) Fabric E strip, sew together the (6) strips as shown. Press the seams open.

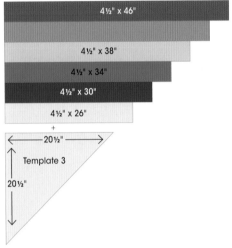

7. Sew a Template 3–Background piece onto the bottom of the unit. Attach the Template 3 piece along the 20½" (52.1cm) edge as shown. Press toward the Template 3 piece.

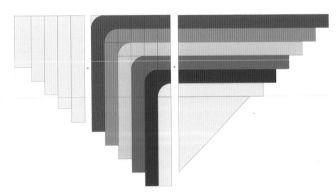

8. Sew together Sections 1, 2, and 3 as shown. Press the seams open and then set it aside.

PIECING SECTION 4

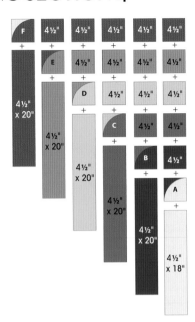

9. Sew together the (6) individual columns as shown. Press the seam open.

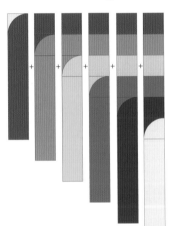

10. Sew the columns together, lining them up at the top of the 4½" x 4½" (11.4 x 11.4cm) Fabric E squares. Press the seams open.

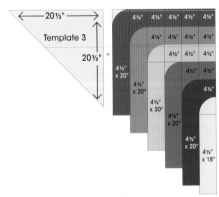

11. Sew a Template 3–Background piece onto the left of the unit. Attach the Template 3 piece along the 20½" (52.1cm) edge as shown. Press toward the Template 3 piece.

PIECING SECTION 5

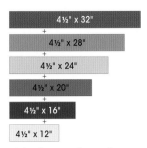

12. Beginning with the 4½" x 32" (11.4 x 81.3cm) Fabric E strip, sew together the (6) strips as shown. Press the seams open.

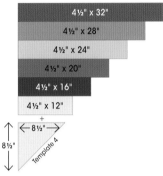

13. Sew a Template 4–Background piece onto the bottom of the unit. Attach the Template 4 piece along the 8½" (21.6cm) edge as shown. Press toward the Template 4 piece.

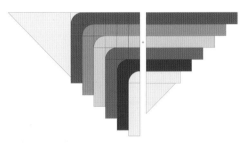

14. Sew Section 4 to the left of Section 5 as shown. Press the seam open.

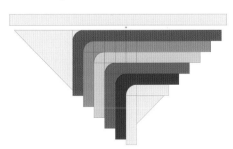

15. Sew (2) 4½" (11.4cm) x WOF Background strips together, creating a 4½" x 82" (11.4 x 208.3cm) Background strip. Press the seam open. Sew the Background strip to the top of the unit as shown. Press toward the Background strip.

QUILT TOP ASSEMBLY

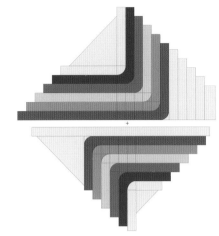

16. Fold both halves of the quilt top in half to mark their centers. Sew them together, lining them up at their marked centers. Press toward the 4½" x 82" (11.4 x 208.3cm) Background strip.

17. Trim the quilt top to 57" x 70" (144.8 x 177.8cm).

FINISHING

18. Make a three-layer quilt sandwich. Make sure the backing piece is at least 2" (5.1cm) larger all the way around the quilt top. Quilt and bind as desired.

Finished Size: 72" x 72" (1.8 x 1.8m)

Skill Level: Intermediate

Fabrics Used: Art Gallery Fabrics in Desert Dunes, Sweet Tangerine, Turmeric, Mirage Blue, Toasty Walnut, Snow, and Magnetism

Pieced by Kelly Stauffer

Longarmed by Mickie Gelling of Wander Stitch Company

MARVELOUS MUSHROOMS QUILT

From the mid-1960s to the mid-1970s, the "back-to-the-land" movement of World War II was revived. This resulted in a substantial number of people migrating from cities to rural areas. The movement was propelled by the motto of "Make Do with Less." There was a desire to not depend on big businesses, machinery, and technology. Inspired by the movement, nature motifs spread into fashion and home décor. One popular motif was the mushroom.

MATERIALS

Yardage is based on 42" (1.1m) wide fabric. Backing assumes at least 4" (10.2cm) coverage on all sides.

Marvelous Mushrooms Templates (page 145)

1 ¼ yards (1.1m) in Fabric A (Red)

¾ yard (68.6cm) in Fabric B (Orange)

1 ¼ yards (1.1m) in Fabric C (Brown)

⅛ yard (11.4cm) in Fabric D (Blue)

⅛ yard (11.4cm) in Fabric E (Yellow)

¼ yard (22.9cm) in Fabric F (White)

5 yards (4.6m) in Background (Gray)

4½ yards (4.1m) in backing fabric

⅝ yard (57.2cm) in binding fabric

82" x 82" (2.1 x 2.1m) in batting

PIECING BLOCK 1

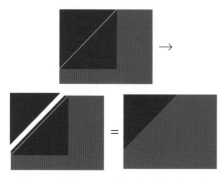

1. Mark a diagonal line on the back of a 4" x 4" (10.2 x 10.2cm) Background square. Place the Background square, RST, in the top left of a 6½" x 8" (16.5 x 20.3cm) Fabric A piece. Sew down the marked line and trim ¼" (6.4mm) away from the sewn line. Press toward the Background piece. Trim to 6½" x 8" (16.5 x 20.3cm).

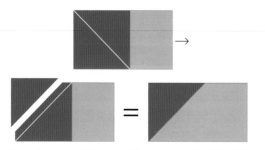

2. Mark a diagonal line on the back of a 2" x 2" (5.1 x 5.1cm) Fabric A square. Place the Fabric A square, RST, in the top left of a 3½" x 2" (8.9 x 5.1cm) Fabric B piece. Sew down the marked line and trim ¼" (6.4mm) away from the sewn line. Press toward the Fabric A piece.

3. Mark a diagonal line on the back of a 2" x 2" (5.1 x 5.1cm) Fabric A square. Place the Fabric A square, RST, in the top right of the unit. Trim to 3½" x 2" (8.9 x 5.1cm). Sew down the marked line and trim ¼" (6.4mm) away from the sewn line. Press toward the Fabric A piece. This creates a Flying Geese block. Make (3) Flying Geese blocks total.

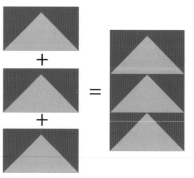

4. Sew the (3) 3½" x 2" (8.9 x 5.1cm) Flying Geese blocks together into a column as shown. Press the seams open.

CUTTING

All templates include a ¼" (6.4mm) seam allowance.

FROM FABRIC A (RED), CUT:

- (3) 6½" (16.5cm) x WOF strips, subcut:
  - (3) 6½" x 8" (16.5 x 20.3cm) rectangles
  - (3) 6½" x 5½" (16.5 x 14cm) rectangles
  - (3) 6½" x 5" (16.5 x 12.7cm) rectangles
  - (3) 6½" x 4½" (16.5 x 11.4cm) rectangles
- (2) 3½" (8.9cm) x WOF strip, subcut:
  - (9) 3½" x 2" (8.9 x 5.1cm) rectangles
  - (3) 3½" x 3½" (8.9 x 8.9cm) squares
  - (3) 3½" x 8½" (8.9 x 21.6cm) strips
- (1) 2¾" (7cm) x WOF strips, subcut:
  - (3) 2¾" x 16½" (7 x 41.9cm) strips
- (3) 2½" (6.4cm) x WOF strips, subcut:
  - (24) 2½" x 2½" (6.4 x 6.4cm) squares
- (1) 2" (5.1cm) x WOF strip, subcut:
  - (18) 2" x 2" (5.1 x 5.1cm)
- (4) 1½" (3.8cm) x WOF strips, subcut:
  - (6) 1½" x 4½" (3.8 x 11.4cm) strips
  - (6) 1½" x 4" (3.8 x 10.2cm) strips
  - (6) 1½" x 2½" (3.8 x 6.4cm) rectangles
  - (39) 1½" x 1½" (3.8 x 3.8cm) squares

FROM FABRIC B (ORANGE), CUT:

- (2) 5½" (14cm) x WOF strips, subcut:
  - (12) Template 1
- (1) 3½" (8.9cm) x WOF strips, subcut:
  - (9) 3½" x 2" (8.9 x 5.1cm) rectangles
- (1) 3" (7.6cm) x WOF strips, subcut:
  - (12) 3" x 1½" (7.6 x 3.8cm) rectangles

FROM FABRIC C (BROWN), CUT:

- (1) 6½" (16.5cm) x WOF strip, subcut:
  - (3) 6½" x 4½" (16.5 x 11.4cm) rectangles
  - (3) 6½" x 2½" (16.5 x 6.4cm) strips
- (2) 5½" (14cm) x WOF strips, subcut:
  - (3) 5½" x 7½" (14 x 19.1cm) rectangles
  - (3) 5½" x 6½" (14 x 16.5cm) rectangles
  - (3) 5½" x 4½" (14 x 11.4cm) rectangles
- (1) 4½" (11.4cm) x WOF strip, subcut:
  - (3) 4½" x 7" (11.4 x 17.8cm) strips
- (1) 3½" (8.9cm) x WOF strip, subcut:
  - (3) 3½" x 4½" (8.9 x 11.4cm) rectangles
- (1) 3" (7.6cm) x WOF strip, subcut:
  - (6) 3" x 6" (7.6 x 15.2cm) strips
- (1) 2½" (6.4cm) x WOF strip, subcut:
  - (6) 2½" x 4½" (6.4 x 11.4cm) rectangles
  - (6) 2½" x 1½" (6.4 x 3.8cm) rectangles
- (3) 1½" (3.8cm) x WOF strips, subcut:
  - (3) 1½" x 14½" (3.8 x 36.8cm) strips
  - (6) 1½" x 4" (3.8 x 10.2cm) strips
  - (6) 1½" x 3½" (3.8 x 8.9cm) rectangles
  - (6) 1½" x 3" (3.8 x 7.6cm) rectangles
  - (12) 1½" x 1½" (3.8 x 3.8cm) squares
- (1) 1" (2.5cm) x WOF strip, subcut:
  - (3) 1" x 4½" (2.5 x 11.4cm) strips

FROM FABRIC D (BLUE), CUT:

- (6) 1" x 4½" (2.5 x 11.4cm) strips

FROM FABRIC E (YELLOW), CUT:

- (6) 3½" x 3½" (8.9 x 8.9cm) squares
- (9) 2" x 2" (5.1 x 5.1cm) squares

FROM FABRIC F (WHITE), CUT:

- (2) 2" (5.1cm) x WOF strips, subcut:
  - (36) 2" x 2" (5.1 x 5.1cm) squares
- (1) 1½" (3.8cm) x WOF strip, subcut:
  - (18) 1½" x 1½" (3.8 x 3.8cm) squares

FROM BACKGROUND (GRAY), CUT:

- (1) 7½" (19.1cm) x WOF strip, subcut:
  - (3) 7½" x 12½" (19.1 x 31.8cm) rectangles
- (2) 6¾" (17.1cm) X WOF strips, subcut:
  - (3) 6¾" x 12½" (17.1 x 31.8cm) strips
  - (3) 6¾" x 8" (17.1 x 20.3cm) rectangles
  - (3) 6¾" x 2¼" (17.1 x 5.7cm) strips
- (2) 6¼" (15.9cm) x WOF strips, subcut:
  - (3) 6¼" x 16½" (15.9 x 41.9cm) strips
- (5) 6" (15.2cm) x WOF strips, subcut:
  - (6) 6" x 8½" (15.2 x 21.6cm) rectangles
  - (12) Template 2
- (2) 5" (12.7cm) x WOF strips, subcut:
  - (6) 5" x 8½" (12.7 x 21.6cm) strips
- (5) 4" (10.2cm) x WOF strips, subcut:
  - (6) 4" x 5" (10.2 x 12.7cm) rectangles
  - (24) 4" x 4" (10.2 x 10.2cm) squares
- (14) 3½" (8.9cm) x WOF strips, subcut:
  - (3) 3½" x 10½" (8.9 x 26.7cm) strips
  - (9) 3½" x 3½" (8.9 x 8.9cm) squares
- (2) 3" (7.6cm) x WOF strips, subcut:
  - (6) 3" x 6" (7.6 x 15.2cm) strips
  - (6) 3" x 5½" (7.6 x 14cm) rectangles
  - (6) 3" x 3½" (7.6 x 8.9cm) rectangles
- (1) 2¾" (7cm) x WOF strips, subcut:
  - (6) 2¾" x 2¾" (7 x 7cm) squares
- (3) 2" (5.1cm) x WOF strips, subcut:
  - (36) 2" x 2" (5.1 x 5.1cm) squares
- (4) 1½" (3.8cm) x WOF strips, subcut:
  - (3) 1½" x 10½" (3.8 x 26.7cm) strips
  - (6) 1½" x 8½" (3.8 x 21.6cm) strips
  - (48) 1½" x 1½" (3.8 x 3.8cm) squares

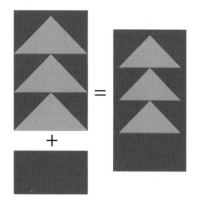

5. Sew 3½" x 2" (8.9 x 5.1cm) Fabric A piece to the bottom of the Flying Geese unit and press toward the Fabric A piece.

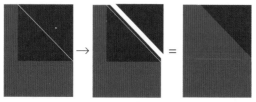

6. Mark a diagonal line on the back of a 4" x 4" (10.2 x 10.2cm) Background square. Place the Background square, RST, in the top right of a 6½" x 5" (16.5 x 12.7cm) Fabric A piece. Sew down the marked line and trim ¼" (6.4mm) away from the sewn line. Press toward the Background piece. Trim to 6½" x 5" (16.5 x 12.7cm).

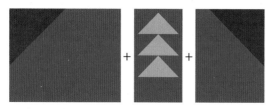

7. Sew the 6½" x 8" (16.5 x 20.3cm) unit to the left of the Flying Geese unit. Sew the 6½" x 5" (16.5 x 12.7cm) unit to the right of the Flying Geese unit. Press toward the Fabric A pieces. Set aside.

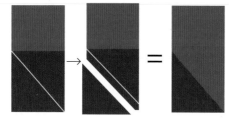

8. Mark a diagonal line on the back of a 1½" x 1½" (3.8 x 3.8cm) Background square. Place the Background square, RST, in the bottom left of a 1½" x 2½" (3.8 x 6.4cm) Fabric A piece. Sew down the marked line and trim ¼" (6.4mm) away from the sewn line. Press toward the Background piece. Trim to 1½" x 2½" (3.8 x 6.4cm).

9. Mark a diagonal line on the back of a 1½" x 1½" (3.8 x 3.8cm) Fabric A square. Place the Fabric A square, RST, in the bottom left of a 1½" x 4" (3.8 x 10.2cm) Fabric C piece. Sew down the marked line and trim ¼" (6.4mm) away from the sewn line. Press toward the Fabric A piece. Trim to 1½" x 4" (3.8 x 10.2cm).

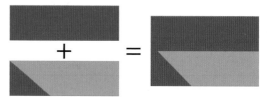

10. Sew a 1½" x 4" (3.8 x 10.2cm) Fabric A piece to the top of the unit. Press toward the Fabric A piece.

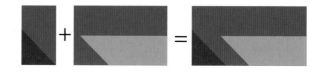

11. Sew the 1½" x 2½" (3.8 x 6.4cm) unit to the left of the unit as shown. Press the seam open.

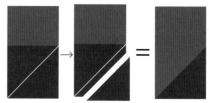

12. Mark a diagonal line on the back of a 1½" x 1½" (3.8 x 3.8cm) Background square. Place the Background square, RST, in the bottom right of a 1½" x 2½" (3.8 x 6.4cm) Fabric A piece. Sew down the marked line and trim ¼" (6.4mm) away from the sewn line. Press toward the Background piece. Trim to 1½" x 2½" (3.8 x 6.4cm).

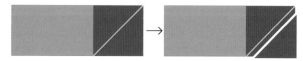

13. Mark a diagonal line on the back of a 1½" x 1½" (3.8 x 3.8cm) Fabric A square. Place the Fabric A square, RST, in the bottom right of a 1½" x 4" (3.8 x 10.2cm) Fabric C piece. Sew down the marked line and trim ¼" (6.4mm) away from the sewn line. Press toward the Fabric A piece.

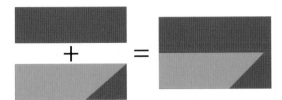

14. Sew a 1½" x 4" (3.8 x 10.2cm) Fabric A piece to the top of the unit. Press toward the Fabric A piece.

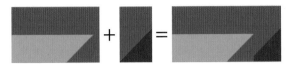

15. Sew the 1½" x 2½" (3.8 x 6.4cm) unit to the right of the unit as shown. Press the seam open.

16. Mark a diagonal line on the back of (2) 1½" x 1½" (3.8 x 3.8cm) Fabric A squares. Place the Fabric A squares, RST, in the top corners of a 6½" x 2½" (16.5 x 6.4cm) Fabric C piece as shown. Sew down the marked lines and trim ¼" (6.4mm) away from the sewn lines. Press toward the Fabric A pieces.

17. Sew the units from steps 11, 15, and 16 together as shown.

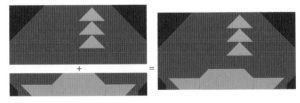

18. Sew the unit completed in step 7 to the top of the unit completed in step 17. Press the seam toward the top unit.

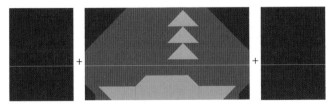

19. Sew a 6" x 8½" (15.2 x 21.6cm) Background piece to each side of the unit. Press toward the Background pieces. Set aside.

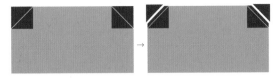

20. Mark a diagonal line on the back of (2) 1½" x 1½" (3.8 x 3.8cm) Background squares. Place the Background squares, RST, in the top corners of a 6½" x 4½" (16.5 x 11.4cm) Fabric C piece as shown. Sew down the marked lines and trim ¼" (6.4mm) away from the sewn lines. Press toward the Background pieces.

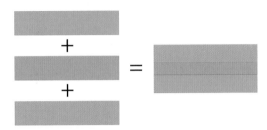

21. Sew a 1" x 4½" (2.5 x 11.4cm) Fabric D piece to the top and to the bottom of a 1" x 4½" (2.5 x 11.4cm) Fabric C piece. Press the seams open.

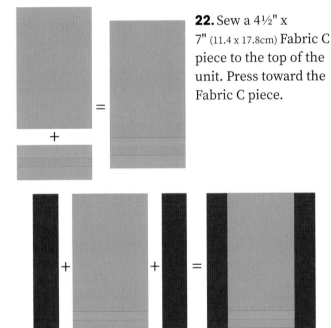

22. Sew a 4½" x 7" (11.4 x 17.8cm) Fabric C piece to the top of the unit. Press toward the Fabric C piece.

23. Sew a 1½" x 8½" (3.8 x 21.6cm) Background piece to either side of the unit. Press toward the Background pieces.

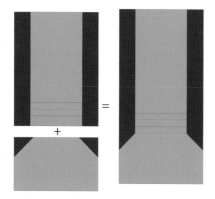

24. Sew the completed unit to the top of the unit made in step 20 as shown. Press the seam open. Set aside.

25. Place a Template 2–Background piece, RST, with a Template 1–Fabric B piece as shown. Sew the pieces together, gently nesting the Template 2 piece into the curve of the Template 1 piece. Use the curve method of your choice (pages 9–10). Square the block to 5½" x 5½" (14 x 14cm) square. This makes the Drunkard's Path block. Make (4) Drunkard's Path blocks total.

26. Mark a diagonal line on the back of a 1½" x 1½" (3.8 x 3.8cm) Background square. Place the Background square, RST, on the left side of a 3" x 1½" (7.6 x 3.8cm) Fabric B piece as shown. Sew down the marked line and trim ¼" (6.4mm) away from the sewn line. Press toward the Background piece.

27. Mark a diagonal line on the back of a 1½" x 1½" (3.8 x 3.8cm) Fabric C square. Place the Fabric C square, RST, on the right side of the unit as shown. Sew down the marked line and trim ¼" (6.4mm) away from the sewn line. Press toward the Fabric C piece. Make (2) of these units.

28. Mark a diagonal line on the back of a 1½" x 1½" (3.8 x 3.8cm) Background square. Place the Background square, RST, on the right side of a 3" x 1½" (7.6 x 3.8cm) Fabric B piece as shown. Sew down the marked line and trim ¼" (6.4mm) away from the sewn line. Press toward the Background piece.

29. Mark a diagonal line on the back of a 1½" x 1½" (3.8 x 3.8cm) Fabric C square. Place the Fabric C square, RST, on the left side of the unit as shown. Sew down the marked line and trim ¼" (6.4mm) away from the sewn line. Press toward the Fabric C piece. Make (2) of these units.

30. Mark a diagonal line on the back of (4) 1½" x 1½" (3.8 x 3.8cm) Background squares. Place (2) Background squares, RST, in the bottom corners of a 5½" x 4½" (14 x 11.4cm) Fabric C piece as shown. Sew down the marked lines and trim ¼" (6.4mm) away from the sewn lines. Press toward the Background pieces.

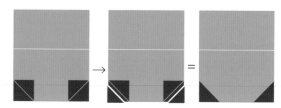

31. Place the remaining (2) marked Background squares in the bottom corners of the 5½" x 6½" (14 x 16.5cm) Fabric C piece as shown. Sew down the marked line and trim ¼" (6.4mm) away from the sewn lines. Press toward the Background pieces.

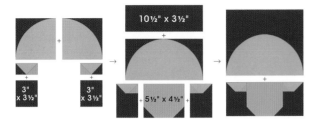

Left Mushroom Assembly Diagram

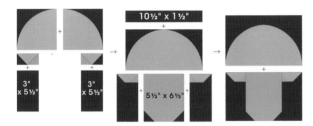

Right Mushroom Assembly Diagram

32. Using the Left Mushroom and Right Mushroom Assembly Diagrams, piece together the small mushrooms for Block 1. Press all seams toward the Background pieces.

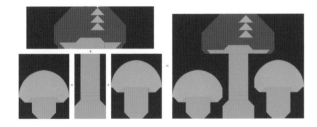

Block 1 Assembly Diagram

33. Using all the completed units made in steps 1–32, use the Block 1 Assembly Diagram to assemble the block. Block 1 finishes at 26½" x 20½" (67.3 x 52.1cm). Make (3) Block 1s total.

PIECING BLOCK 2

34. Mark a diagonal line on the back of (2) 2¾" x 2¾" (7 x 7cm) Background squares. Place the Background squares, RST, on both ends of a 2¾" x 16½" (7 x 41.9cm) Fabric A piece as shown. Sew down the marked line and trim ¼" (6.4mm) away from the sewn line. Press toward the Background piece.

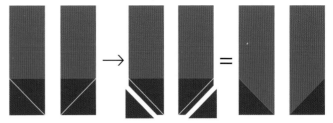

35. Mark a diagonal line on the back of (2) 1½" x 1½" (3.8 x 3.8cm) Background squares. Place (1) marked Background square each, RST, on the bottom of (2) 1½" x 4½" (3.8 x 11.4cm) Fabric A pieces as shown. Sew down the marked line and trim ¼" (6.4mm) away from the sewn line. Press toward the Background piece.

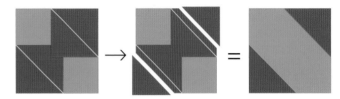

36. Mark a diagonal line on the back of (4) 2½" x 2½" (6.4 x 6.4cm) Fabric A squares. Place (2) Fabric A squares, RST, in opposing corners of a 3½" x 3½" (8.9 x 8.9cm) Fabric E square as shown. Sew down the marked lines and trim ¼" (6.4mm) away from the sewn lines. Press toward the Fabric A pieces.

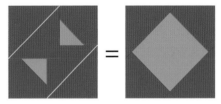

37. Place the remaining (2) marked Fabric A squares, RST, in the open opposing corners as shown. Sew down the marked lines and trim ¼" (6.4mm) away from the sewn lines. Press toward the Fabric A pieces. This creates the Economy block. Make (2) Economy blocks.

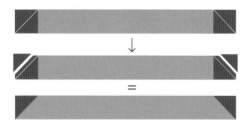

38. Mark a diagonal line on the back of (2) 1½" x 1½" (3.8 x 3.8cm) Fabric A squares. Place each marked Fabric A square, RST, on the end of a 1½" x 14½" (3.8 x 36.8cm) Fabric C piece as shown. Sew down the marked lines and trim ¼" (6.4mm) away from the sewn lines. Press toward the Fabric A pieces.

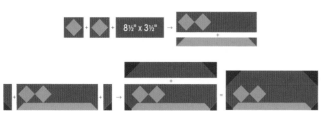

Block 2 Mushroom Top Assembly Diagram

39. Use the Block 2 Mushroom Top Assembly Diagram and the units from steps 34–38 to piece the top of Block 2. Press the seams open. Set aside.

40. Sew a 1½" x 1½" (3.8 x 3.8cm) Fabric F square to the right of a 2½" x 1½" (6.4 x 3.8cm) Fabric C piece as shown. Make (2) units.

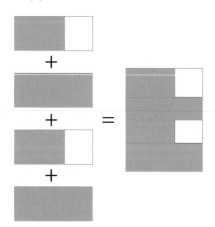

41. Sew the (2) units and (2) 1½" x 3½" (3.8 x 8.9cm) Fabric C pieces together, alternating as shown. Press toward the 3½" x 1½" (8.9 x 3.8cm) Fabric C pieces.

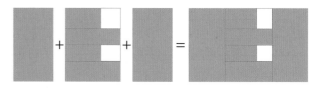

42. Sew a 2½" x 4½" (6.4 x 11.4cm) Fabric C piece onto each side of the unit as shown. Press toward the Fabric C piece.

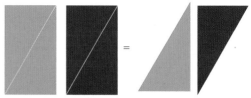

43. To create the left-side half-rectangle triangle (HRT), mark a diagonal line on the back of a 3" x 6" (7.6 x 15.2cm) Fabric C piece and a 3" x 6" (7.6 x 15.2cm) Background piece as shown. Cut along the marked line.

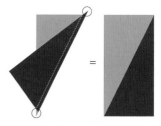

44. Place the HRT–Background, RST, with the HRT–Color C as shown, leaving a ¼" (6.4mm) overhang off each point. Sew together ¼" (6.4mm) away from the long edge. Press toward the Background piece.

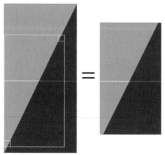

45. Trim the HRT to 2½" x 4½" (6.4 x 11.4cm). Make sure that the diagonal seam line does not go corner to corner but ¼" (6.4mm) from the end on both sides.

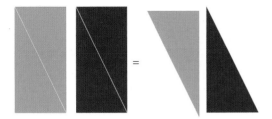

46. To create the right-side HRT, mark a diagonal line on the back of a 3" x 6" (7.6 x 15.2cm) Fabric C piece and a 3" x 6" (7.6 x 15.2cm) Background piece as shown. Cut along the marked line.

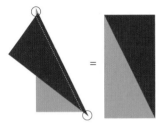

47. Place the HRT–Background, RST, with the HRT–Color C as shown, leaving a ¼" (6.4mm) overhang off each point. Sew together ¼" (6.4mm) away from the long edge. Press toward the Background piece. Trim as shown in step 45.

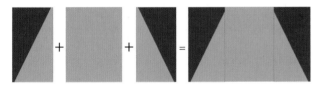

48. Sew an HRT to each side of a 3½" x 4½" (8.9 x 11.4cm) Fabric C piece as shown. Press toward the Fabric C piece.

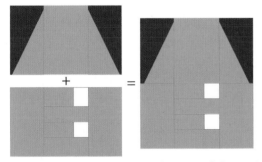

49. Sew the completed unit to the top of the unit completed in step 42. Press toward the top unit.

50. Sew a 5" x 8½" (12.7 x 21.6cm) Background piece to each side of the completed unit. Press toward the Background pieces. This completes the bottom of Block 2.

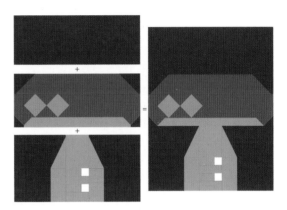

Block 2 Assembly Diagram

51. Sew the top of Block 2 from step 39 to the bottom of Block 2 from step 50. Press the seam open. Sew a 6¼" x 16½" (15.9 x 41.9cm) Background piece to the top of the unit. Press toward the Background piece. Block 2 finishes at 16½" x 20" (41.9 x 50.8cm). Make (3) Block 2s total.

PIECING BLOCK 3

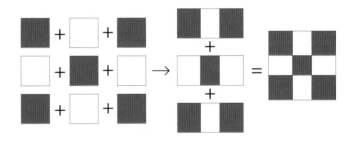

52. Sew a Nine Patch block using (5) 1½" x 1½" (3.8 x 3.8cm) Fabric A squares and (4) 1½" x 1½" (3.8 x 3.8cm) Fabric F squares as shown. Press the seams open.

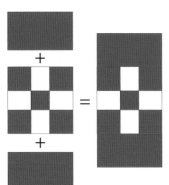

53. Sew a 3½" x 2" (8.9 x 5.1cm) Fabric A piece to the top and to the bottom of the Nine Patch block. Press toward the Fabric A pieces.

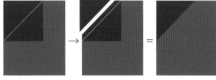

54. Mark a diagonal line on the back of a 3½" x 3½" (8.9 x 8.9cm) Background square. Place the Background square, RST, in the top left of a 6½" x 5½" (16.5 x 14cm) Fabric A piece as shown. Sew down the marked line and trim ¼" (6.4mm) away from the sewn line. Press toward the Background piece.

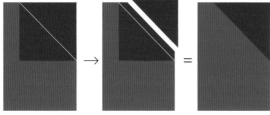

55. Mark a diagonal line on the back of a 3½" x 3½" (8.9 x 8.9cm) Background square. Place the Background square, RST, in the top right of a 6½" x 4½" (16.5 x 11.4cm) Fabric A piece as shown. Sew down the marked line and trim ¼" (6.4mm) away from the sewn line. Press toward the Background piece.

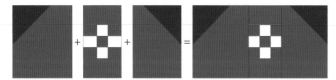

56. Sew the 6½" x 5½" (16.5 x 14cm) unit to the left of the Nine Patch unit. Sew the 6½" x 4½" (16.5 x 11.4cm) unit to the right of the Nine Patch unit. Press the seams toward the side pieces. This completes the top of Block 3. Set aside.

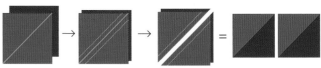

57. Mark a diagonal line on the back of a 3½" x 3½" (8.9 x 8.9cm) Fabric A square. Place the Fabric A square, RST, with a 3½" x 3½" (8.9 x 8.9cm) Background square. Sew ¼" (6.4mm) away from the marked line on both sides. Cut down the marked line and press toward the Background fabric. Square the (2) HSTs to 3" x 3" (7.6 x 7.6cm).

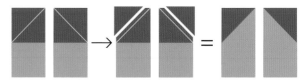

58. Mark a diagonal line on the back of (2) 1½" x 1½" (3.8 x 3.8cm) Fabric A squares. Place (1) marked Fabric A square each, RST, on the bottom of (2) 1½" x 3" (3.8 x 7.6cm) Fabric C pieces as shown. Sew down the marked lines and trim ¼" (6.4mm) away from the sewn lines. Press toward the Fabric A pieces.

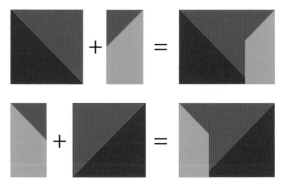

59. Sew the completed units to the HSTs as shown. Press the seams open.

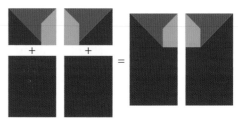

60. Sew (1) 4" x 5" (10.2 x 12.7) Background piece to the bottom of each unit as shown. Press toward the Background piece.

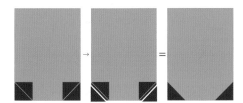

61. Mark a diagonal line on the back of (2) 1½" x 1½" (3.8 x 3.8cm) Background squares. Place the marked Background squares, RST, on the bottom of a 5½" x 7½" (14 x 19.1cm) Fabric C piece as shown. Sew down the marked lines and trim ¼" (6.4mm) away from the sewn lines. Press toward the Background pieces.

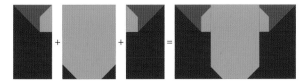

62. Sew the units completed in step 60 to the unit as shown. This completes the bottom of Block 3.

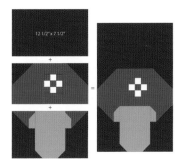

Block 3 Assembly Diagram

63. Sew the top of Block 3 from step 56 to the bottom of Block 3 from step 62. Press the seam open. Sew a 12½" x 7½" (31.8 x 19.1cm) Background piece to the top of the unit. Press toward the Background piece. Block 3 finishes at 12½" x 20½" (31.8 x 52.1cm). Make (3) Block 3s total.

PIECING THE FLOWER BLOCK

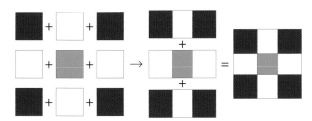

64. Sew a Nine Patch block using (1) 2" x 2" (5.1 x 5.1cm) Fabric E square, (4) 2" x 2" (5.1 x 5.1cm) Fabric F squares, and (4) 2" x 2" (5.1 x 5.1cm) Background squares as shown. Press the seams open.

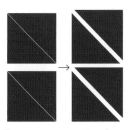

65. Cut (2) 4" x 4" (10.2 x 10.2cm) Background squares in half diagonally, creating (4) triangles.

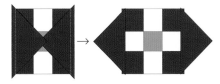

66. Place (2) Background triangles, RST, with the Nine Patch block. Sew on opposing sides as shown. Press toward the Background triangles.

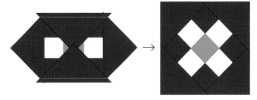

67. Place the (2) remaining Background triangles, RST, on the remaining opposing sides and sew. Press toward the Background triangles. The Flower block finishes at 6¾" x 6¾" (17.1 x 17.1cm) square. Make (9) Flower blocks total.

PIECING BLOCK 4

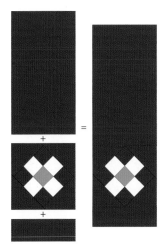

68. Sew a 6¾" x 12½" (17.1 x 31.8cm) Background block to the top of a Flower block. Sew a 6¾" x 2¼" (17.1 x 5.7cm) Background piece to the bottom of the Flower block. Press toward the Background pieces. Make (3) Block 4s total.

PIECING BLOCK 5

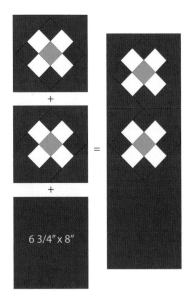

69. Sew (2) Flower blocks together and press the seam open. Sew (1) 6¾" x 8" (17.1 x 20.3cm) Background piece to the bottom of the Flower unit as shown. Press toward the Background piece. Make (3) Block 5s total.

QUILT TOP ASSEMBLY

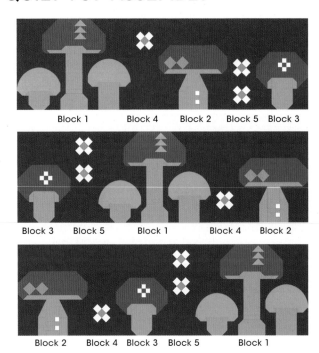

Marvelous Mushrooms Rows Assembly Diagram

70. Use the Marvelous Mushrooms Rows Assembly Diagram to piece together the quilt top rows. Blocks 4 and 5 rotate throughout the quilt.

71. Use the (12) 3½" (8.9cm) x WOF Background strips for the sashing and borders. Sew them together in pairs of two, creating (6) strips. Trim (4) of the strips to 3½" x 68½" (8.9 x 174cm). Sew (1) 3½" x 68½" (8.9 x 174cm) Background strip between each row of blocks, joining the rows together. Press toward the Background strips.

72. Sew (2) 3½" x 68½" (8.9 x 174cm) Background strips to the top and bottom of the quilt top. Press toward the borders.

73. Trim the (2) remaining strip units from step 71 to 3½" x 72" (8.9 x 182.9cm). Sew (1) strip onto each side of the quilt top. Press toward the borders.

FINISHING

74. Make a three-layer quilt sandwich. Make sure the backing piece is at least 2" (5.1cm) larger all the way around the quilt top. Quilt and bind as desired.

Finished Size: 52" x 60" (1.3 x 1.5m)

Skill Level: Intermediate

Fabrics Used: Art Gallery Fabrics Pure Solids Turmeric, Patina Green, Crystal Pink, Cozumel Blue, White Linen, and Magnetism

Pieced by Kelly Stauffer

Quilted by Mickie Gelling of Wander Stitch Company

POSITIVELY PYREX QUILT

Pyrex mixing bowl sets were a common wedding gift during the 1960s through the 1970s. They were known for their vibrant array of colors and patterns on revolutionary kitchenware that could go straight from the oven to the dinner table then into the fridge. The colorful kitchenware has made a comeback and is sought out at thrift and antique stores across the nation. I'm a proud owner of a full rainbow collection of traditional and princess bowl sets.

MATERIALS

Yardage is based on 42" (1.1m) wide fabric. Backing assumes at least 4" (10.2cm) coverage on all sides.

Positively Pyrex Templates (pages 146–147)

⅓ yard (30.5cm) in Fabric A (Blue)

½ yard (45.7cm) in Fabric B (Green)

¼ yard (22.9cm) in Fabric C (Pink)

¼ yard (22.9cm) in Fabric D (Yellow)

1 yard (91.4cm) in Fabric E (Cream)

4 yards (3.7m) in Background (Gray)

4 yards (3.7m) in backing fabric

½ yard (45.7cm) in binding fabric

62" x 70" (1.6 x 1.8m) in batting

CUTTING

All templates include a ¼" (6.4mm) seam allowance.

FROM FABRIC A (BLUE), CUT:

(2) 2" (5.1cm) x WOF strips

(1) 1½" (3.8cm) x WOF strips

(4) 402A Templates

FROM FABRIC B (GREEN), CUT:

(6) Template 404A

(6) Template 402A

(3) Sets of small Crazy Daisies Appliqué

FROM FABRIC C (PINK), CUT:

(4) Template 404A

(4) Template 402A

(2) Sets of small Sprout Appliqué

FROM FABRIC D (YELLOW), CUT:

(4) Template 404A

(4) Template 402A

FROM FABRIC E (CREAM), CUT:

(2) 2" (5.1cm) x WOF strips

(3) 5½" (14cm) x WOF strips, subcut:
(18) Template 403A

(2) 2½" (6.4cm) x WOF strips, subcut:
(18) Template 401A

(3) Sets of large Crazy Daisies Appliqué

(2) Sets of large Sprout Appliqué

(2) Sets of Full Bloom Appliqué

FROM BACKGROUND (GRAY), CUT:

(4) 7¾" (19.7cm) x WOF strips, subcut:
(18) Template 404B

(5) 7" (17.8cm) x WOF strips, subcut:
(9) 7" x 18" (17.8 x 45.7cm) strips

(3) 5¾" (14.6cm) x WOF strips, subcut:

(18) Template 403B

(2) 3¾" (9.5cm) x WOF strips, subcut:
(18) Template 402B

(2) 2¾" (7cm) x WOF strips, subcut:
(18) Template 401B

(10) 2½" (6.4cm) x WOF strips, subcut:
(18) 2½" x 14" (6.4 x 35.6cm) strips
(18) 2½" x 3½" (6.4 x 8.9cm) rectangles
(18) 2½" x 4½" (6.4 x 11.4cm) rectangles

(3) 2" (5.1cm) x WOF strips, subcut:
(18) 2" x 5½" (5.1 x 14cm) rectangles

PIECING THE STRIPED BOWL BLOCK

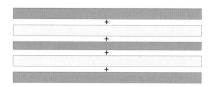

1. Piece together (2) 2" (5.1cm) x WOF Fabric A strips, (2) 2" (5.1cm) x WOF Fabric E strips, and (1) 1½" (3.8cm) x WOF Fabric A strips as shown in the diagram. Press the seams open.

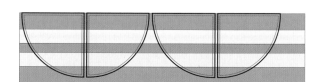

2. Place Template 404A on top of the stripe unit. Line the template up with the top of the stripe unit. Cut out (4) Template 404As from the stripe unit. **NOTE:** Play close attention to the directionality of the template.

3. Place a Template 404B–Background piece, RST, with the Template 404A–stripe unit as shown. Sew the pieces together, gently nesting the Template 404B piece into the curve of the Template 404A piece. Use the curve method of your choice (pages 9–10). Press toward the Template 404B piece. Square the Drunkard's Path block to 7½" x 7½" (19.1 x 19.1cm).

4. Repeat step 3 with the remaining stripe units and Template 404A pieces. Make (4) Drunkard's Path blocks total.

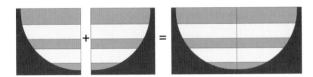

5. Sew together the left-facing block with the right-facing block. Press the seam open. This will make (2) Striped Bowl blocks.

PIECING THE LARGE BOWL BLOCK

6. Place a Template 404B–Background piece, RST, with a Template 404A–Fabric B piece as shown. Sew the pieces together, gently nesting the Template 404B piece into the curve of the Template 404A piece. Press toward the Template 404B piece. Square the block to 7½" x 7½" (19.1 x 19.1cm).

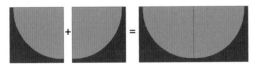

7. Repeat step 6 to make (6) Drunkard's Path Fabric B blocks total. Sew together (2) blocks as shown. Press the seam open. This will make a Fabric B Bowl block. Make (3) blocks total.

8. Using raw edge appliqué (page 11), apply the large Crazy Daisies Appliqué pieces in Fabric E to the Fabric B Bowl blocks as shown.

9. Place a Template 404B–Background piece, RST, with a Template 404A–Fabric C piece. Sew the pieces together, gently nesting the Template 404B piece into the curve of the Template 404A piece. Press toward the Template 404B piece. Square the block to 7½" x 7½" (19.1 x 19.1cm).

10. Repeat step 9 to make (4) Drunkard's Path Fabric C blocks total. Sew together (2) blocks as shown. Press the seam open. This will make a Fabric C Bowl block. Make (2) blocks total.

11. Using raw edge appliqué, apply the large Sprout Appliqué templates in Fabric E to the Fabric C Bowl blocks as shown.

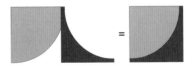

12. Place a Template 404B–Background piece, RST, with a Template 404A–Fabric D piece. Sew the pieces together, gently nesting the Template 404B piece into the curve of the Template 404A piece. Press toward the Template 404B piece. Square the block to 7½" x 7½" (19.1 x 19.1cm).

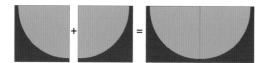

13. Repeat step 12 to make (4) Drunkard's Path Fabric D blocks total. Sew together (2) blocks as shown. Press the seam open. This will make a Fabric D Bowl block. Make (2) blocks total.

14. Using raw edge appliqué, apply the Full Bloom Appliqué templates in Fabric E to the Fabric D Bowl blocks as shown.

PIECING THE MEDIUM BOWL BLOCK

15. Place a Template 403B–Background piece, RST, with a Template 403A–Fabric E piece. Sew the pieces together, gently nesting the Template 403B piece into the curve of the Template 403A piece. Press toward the Template 403B piece. Square the block to 5½" x 5½" (14 x 14cm).

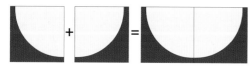

16. Repeat step 15 to make (18) Drunkard's Path Fabric E blocks total. Sew together (2) blocks as shown. Press the seam open. Make (9) units total.

17. Trim each unit to 10½" x 3½" (26.7 x 8.9cm), removing 2" (5.1cm) from the bottom of the unit.

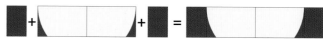

18. Sew a 2½" x 3½" (6.4 x 8.9cm) Background piece to both sides of the unit. Press toward the Background piece. This will yield (9) Medium Bowl blocks.

19. Using raw edge appliqué, apply the small Crazy Daisies Appliqué templates in Fabric B to (3) Medium Bowl blocks as shown.

20. Using raw edge appliqué, apply the small Sprout Appliqué templates in Fabric C to (2) Medium Bowl blocks as shown. The remaining (4) Medium Bowl blocks do not have appliqué pieces.

PIECING THE SMALL BOWL BLOCK

21. Place a Template 402B–Background piece, RST, with a Template 402A–Fabric A piece. Sew the pieces together, gently nesting the Template 402B piece into the curve of the Template 402A piece. Press toward the Template 402B piece. Square the Drunkard's Path block to 3½" x 3½" (8.9 x 8.9cm). Make (4) Drunkard's Path Fabric A blocks total.

22. Place a Template 402B–Background piece, RST, with a Template 402A–Fabric B piece. Sew the pieces together, gently nesting the Template 402B piece into the curve of the Template 402A piece. Press toward the Template 402B piece. Square the Drunkard's Path block to 3½" x 3½" (8.9 x 8.9cm). Make (6) Drunkard's Path Fabric B blocks total.

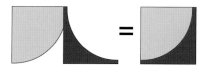

23. Place a Template 402B–Background piece, RST, with a Template 402A–Fabric C piece. Sew the pieces together, gently nesting the Template 402B piece into the curve of the Template 402A piece. Press toward the Template 402B piece. Square the Drunkard's Path block to 3½" x 3½" (8.9 x 8.9cm). Make (4) Drunkard's Path Fabric C blocks total.

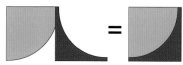

24. Place a Template 402B–Background piece, RST, with a Template 402A–Fabric D piece. Sew the pieces together, gently nesting the Template 402B piece into the curve of the Template 402A piece. Press toward the Template 402B piece. Square the Drunkard's Path block to 3½" x 3½" (8.9 x 8.9cm). Make (4) Drunkard's Path Fabric D blocks total.

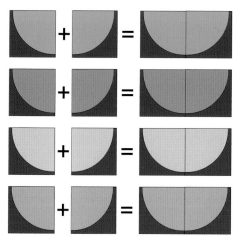

25. Sew (2) coordinating Drunkard's Path blocks together and press the seam open. Repeat for all 3½" x 3½" (8.9 x 8.9cm) Drunkard's Path blocks. Make (9) units total.

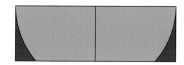

26. Trim each unit to 6½" x 2½" (16.5 x 6.4cm), removing 1" (2.5cm) from the bottom of the unit.

27. Sew a 2½" x 4½" (6.4 x 11.4cm) Background piece to both sides of the unit. Press toward the Background pieces. This will yield (9) Small Bowl blocks.

PIECING THE TINY BOWL BLOCK

28. Place a Template 401B–Background piece, RST, with a Template 401A–Fabric E piece. Sew the pieces together, gently nesting the Template 401B piece into the curve of the Template 401A piece. Press toward the Template 401B piece. Square the Drunkard's Path block to 2½" x 2½" (6.4 x 6.4cm). Make (18) Drunkard's Path Fabric E blocks total.

29. Sew together (2) Drunkard's Path Fabric E blocks as shown. Press the seam open. Make (9) units total.

30. Trim each unit to 4½" x 2" (11.4 x 5.1cm), removing ½" (1.3cm) from the bottom of the unit.

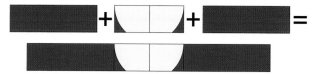

31. Sew a 2" x 5½" (5.1 x 14cm) Background piece to both sides of the unit. Press toward the Background pieces. This will yield (9) Tiny Bowl blocks.

QUILT TOP ASSEMBLY

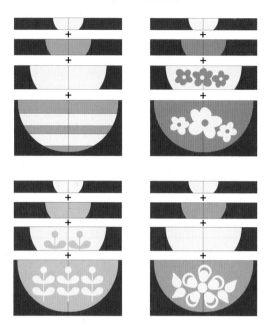

Block Assembly Diagram

32. Use the Block Assembly Diagram to piece (1) of each block in coordinating colors: Large Bowl, Medium Bowl, Small Bowl, and Tiny Bowl. This will yield (2) Fabric A, (3) Fabric B, (2) Fabric C, and (2) Fabric D Bowl blocks.

33. Sew a 2½" x 14" (6.4 x 35.6cm) Background strip to both sides of all the Bowl blocks. Press toward the Background strips.

34. Arrange Bowl blocks and 7" x 18" (17.8 x 45.7cm) Background pieces into (3) individual columns as shown. Sew the columns and press the seams open.

35. Use the Assembly Diagram to assemble the quilt top. Sew the columns together. Press the seams open.

FINISHING

36. Make a three-layer quilt sandwich. Make sure the backing piece is at least 2" (5.1cm) larger all the way around the quilt top. Quilt and bind as desired.

Finished Size: 60" x 60" (1.5 x 1.5m)

Skill Level: Intermediate

Fabrics Use: Art Gallery Fabrics Pure Solids Turmeric, Sweet Tangerine, Mirage Blue, and Creme de la Creme

Pieced & Quilted by Erin Grogan

RETRO BLOOMS QUILT

Retro Blooms was inspired by the mid-century modern interior design movement of the mid-20th century. The furnishings had simple, functional, curved designs. These designs aspired to integrate mass production and the technology of the time with a more optimistic outlook for the future. You can see this emulated in the clean, straight lines of the floral stems and the smooth curves of the blooms within this quilt.

MATERIALS

Yardage is based on 42" (1.1m) wide fabric. Backing assumes at least 4" (10.2cm) coverage on all sides.

Retro Blooms Templates (page 148)

3 yards (2.7m) in Fabric A (Yellow)

2¾ yards (2.5m) in Fabric B (Orange)

1¾ yards (1.6m) in Fabric C (Blue)

3¼ yards (3m) in Fabric D (Cream)

4 yards (3.7m) in backing fabric

½ yard (45.7cm) in binding fabric

70" x 70" (1.8 x 1.8m) in batting

CUTTING

All templates include a ¼" (6.4mm) seam allowance.

FROM FABRIC A (YELLOW), CUT:

(4) 7½" (19.1cm) x WOF strips, subcut:
   (16) Template 2

(4) 8" (20.3cm) x WOF strips, subcut:
   (32) Template 1

(4) 3" (7.6cm) x WOF strips

FROM FABRIC B (ORANGE), CUT:

(3) 5½" (14cm) x WOF strips, subcut:
   (16) Template 3

(4) 8" (20.3cm) x WOF strips, subcut:
   (16) Template 1

(4) 8½" (21.6cm) x WOF strips, subcut:
   (16) Template 6

(4) 2½" (6.4cm) x WOF strips

FROM FABRIC C (BLUE), CUT:

(4) 8½" (21.6cm) x WOF strips, subcut:
   (16) Template 6

(2) 3½" (8.9cm) x WOF strips, subcut:
   (16) Template 4

(4) 3½" (8.9cm) x WOF strips

FROM FABRIC D (CREAM), CUT:

(4) 8" (20.3cm) x WOF strips, subcut:
   (16) Template 1

(8) 7½" (19.1cm) x WOF strips, subcut:
   (48) Template 5

(3) 4½" (11.4cm) x WOF strips, subcut:
   (2) 4½" x 15" (11.4 x 38.1cm) strips

(4) 1" x WOF strips, subcut:
   (16) 1" x 7½" (2.5 x 19.1cm) strips

PIECING BLOCK 1

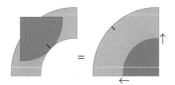

1. Fold a Template 4–Fabric C and Template 3–Fabric B piece in half. Mark their centers. Place the template pieces RST, and pin them together at their marked centers. Line up the template ends and sew the pieces together, working slowly around the curve. Use the curve method of your choice (pages 9–10). Press the seam toward Template 3.

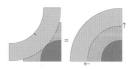

2. Fold the unit in half and mark the center along the Template 3 edge. Fold the Template 2–Fabric A piece in half and mark the center. Line up the Template 2 piece, RST, with the unit at their centers and pin. Line up the ends of the pieces and sew together. Press the seam toward the Template 2 piece.

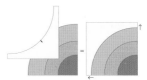

3. Fold a Template 1–Fabric D piece in half and mark the center. Place the Template 1 piece, RST, with the unit, lining up at their centers. Pin together and sew. Press the seam toward the Template 1 piece.

4. Square the block to 7½" x 7½" (19.1 x 19.1cm). This is Block 1. Make (16) Block 1s total.

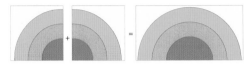

5. Group all Block 1s into groups of (2) as shown. With them RST, line up the seams and sew the blocks together. Press the seams open. This will yield (8) units total.

PIECING BLOCK 2

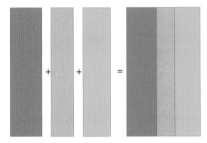

6. Sew together (1) 3½" (8.9cm) x WOF Fabric C strip, (1) 2½" (6.4cm) x WOF Fabric B strip, and (1) 3" (7.6cm) x WOF Fabric A strip as shown. Press the seams open. Make (4) strip sets total.

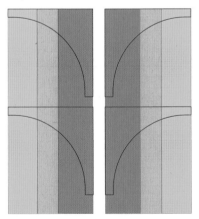

7. Subcut a total of (8) left-facing and (8) right-facing Template 6s from the strip sets as shown. You should be able to cut (4) templates from each strip set. Pay close attention to the template and fabric orientation.

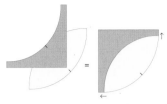

8. Fold a Template 1–Fabric A and Template 5–Fabric D piece in half. Mark their centers. Place the template pieces, RST, lining up at their marked centers on one side. Pin together and sew. Press the seam toward Template 1 piece.

9. Fold a Template 6–strip set piece in half and mark the center. Place the Template 6 piece, RST, with the unit, lining up at their centers. Pin together and sew. Press the seam toward the Template 6 piece.

10. Square the block to 7½" x 7½" (19.1 x 19.1cm). This is Block 2. Make (8) left-facing and (8) right-facing Block 2s total.

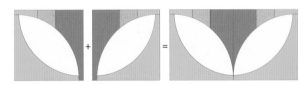

11. Group all Block 2s into groups of (2) as shown. With them RST, line up the seams and sew them together. Press the seams open. This will yield (8) units total.

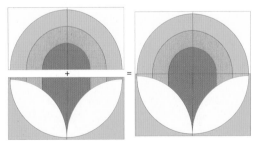

12. Sew together a unit from step 5 with a unit from step 11 as shown. Press the seams open. This completes the Bloom block. Make (8) Bloom blocks total.

PIECING BLOCK 3

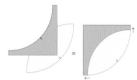

13. Fold a Template 1–Fabric A and Template 5–Fabric D piece in half. Mark their centers. Place the template pieces, RST, lining up at their marked centers on one side. Pin together and sew. Press the seam toward Template 1 piece.

14. Fold a Template 6–Fabric B piece in half and mark the center. Place the Template 6 piece, RST, with the unit, lining up at their centers. Pin together and sew. Press the seam toward the Template 6 piece.

15. Square the block to 7½" x 7½" (19.1 x 19.1cm). This is Block 3. Make (16) Block 3s total.

16. Group all Block 3s into pairs of (2) where the Fabric A pieces are pointing inward and the Fabric B pieces are pointing outward. Trim ¼" (6.4mm) from the Fabric A edge as shown.

17. Join the (2) blocks by sewing (1) 1" x 7½" (2.5 x 19.1cm) Fabric D strip between them. Press toward the Fabric D strip. Make (8) units total.

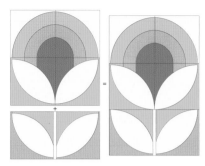

18. Sew the unit to the bottom of the Bloom block completed in step 11. Press the seam open. This will yield (8) units.

PIECING BLOCK 4

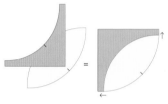

19. Fold a Template 1–Fabric B and Template 5–Fabric D piece in half. Mark their centers. Place the template pieces, RST, lining up at their marked centers on one side. Pin together and sew. Press the seam toward Template 1 piece.

20. Fold a Template 6–Fabric C piece in half and mark the center. Place the Template 6 piece, RST, with the unit, lining up at their centers. Pin together and sew. Press the seam toward the Template 6 piece.

21. Square the block to 7½" x 7½" (19.1 x 19.1cm). This is Block 4. Make (16) Block 4s total.

22. Group all Block 4s into pairs of (2) where the Fabric B pieces are pointing inward and the Fabric C pieces are pointing outward. Trim ¼" (6.4mm) from the Fabric B edge as shown.

23. Join the (2) blocks by sewing (1) 1" x 7½" (2.5 x 19.1cm) Fabric D strip between them. Press toward the Fabric D strip. Make (8) units total.

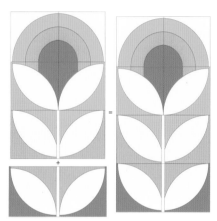

24. Sew the unit to the bottom of the unit completed in step 18. Press the seam open. This will yield (8) units.

QUILT TOP ASSEMBLY

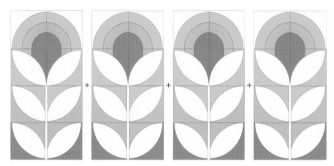

25. Join (4) completed units from step 24. Repeat this step, creating (2) rows as shown.

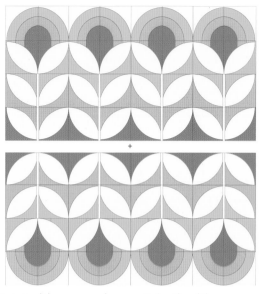

26. Rotate (1) row as shown. Join the (2) rows and press the seams open.

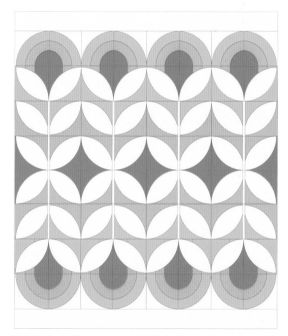

27. Sew (1) 4½" (11.4cm) x WOF Fabric D strip with (1) 4½" x 15" (11.4 x 38.1cm), creating a 4½" x 56½" (11.4 x 143.5cm) Fabric D strip. Press the seam open. Make (2) 4½" x 56½" (11.4 x 143.5cm) strips total. Piece one to the top of the quilt top and one to the bottom, completing the top. Press toward the Fabric D strips.

FINISHING

28. Make a three-layer quilt sandwich. Make sure the backing piece is at least 2" (5.1cm) larger all the way around the quilt top. Quilt and bind as desired.

Finished Size: 65" x 69" (1.7 x 1.8m)

Skill Level: Intermediate

Fabrics Used: Art Gallery Fabrics Pure Solids Raw Gold, Apple Cider, Mandarin, Marmalade, Ruby, Lemonade, Dark Citron, Caviar, and Creme de la Creme

Pieced by Erin Grogan

Quilted by Tami Pugmire

STRAWBERRY FIELDS QUILT

Strawberry Fields, like the Marvelous Mushrooms pattern, was inspired by the "back-to-the-land" movement. You can find owls used in mid-20th century designs from macramé, salt and pepper shakers, and other kitchenware. Just as often as you find owls, you also find strawberries. The little pops of red from the strawberries are a welcome break from the browns and golds of '70s style.

MATERIALS

Yardage is based on 42" (1.1m) wide fabric. Backing assumes at least 4" (10.2cm) coverage on all sides.

Strawberry Fields Templates (pages 149–152)

1¼ yards (1.1m) in Fabric A (Light Brown)

½ yard (45.7cm) in Fabric B (Dark Brown)

⅓ yard (30.5cm) in Fabric C (Light Orange)

¼ yard (22.9cm) in Fabric D (Dark Orange)

1 yard (91.4cm) in Fabric E (Red)

1¼ yards (1.1m) in Fabric F (Light Green)

1¼ yards (1.1m) in Fabric G (Dark Green)

¼ yard (22.9cm) in Fabric H (Black)

3 yards (2.7m) in Background (Cream)

4⅓ yards (4m) in backing fabric

½ yard (45.7cm) in binding fabric

75" x 79" (1.9 x 2m) in batting

PIECING THE STRAWBERRY BLOCK

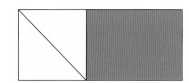

1. Mark a diagonal line on the back of (32) 3" x 3" (7.6 x 7.6cm) Background squares. Place a marked Background square, RST, in the bottom-left corner of a 3" x 6½" (7.6 x 16.5cm) Fabric E rectangle.

4. Mark a diagonal line on the back of (48) 1½" x 1½" (3.8 x 3.8cm) Fabric H squares.

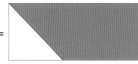

2. Sew down the marked line, then trim ¼" (6.4mm) away from the sewn line. Press toward the Fabric E piece.

5. Place the marked Fabric H square, RST, on the right end of a 1½" x 5½" (3.8 x 14cm) Fabric E strip. Sew down the marked line, and trim ¼" (6.4mm) away from the sewn line. Press toward the Fabric H piece. Make (32) units total.

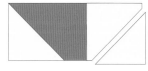
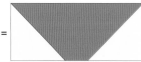

3. Place a marked Background square, RST, in the bottom-right corner of the unit. Sew down the marked line, then trim ¼" (6.4mm) away from the sewn line. Press toward Fabric E piece. Make (16) units total.

6. Sew (1) 1½" x 1½" (3.8 x 3.8cm) Fabric E square to the right side of all units from step 5. Press toward the Fabric E square.

CUTTING

All templates include a ¼" (6.4mm) seam allowance. Mirror image of a template means to turn the template upside down so that the template text is right side touching the fabric.

FROM FABRIC A (LIGHT BROWN), CUT:

- (1) 9½" x 13½" (24.1 x 34.3cm) rectangle
- (1) 8½" x 24" (21.6 x 61cm) rectangle
- (2) Template 1
- (2) Template 2
- (2) Template 7
- (1) Template 10
- (1) Template 10, mirror image
- (1) Template 12
- (1) Template 12, mirror image
- (3) Template 16A
- (3) Template 16B
- (2) 4½" (11.4cm) x WOF strips, subcut:
  - (1) 4½" x 16½" (11.4 x 41.9cm) strip
  - (2) 4½" x 10½" (11.4 x 26.7cm) strips
  - (1) 4½" x 9½" (11.4 x 24.1cm) strip
  - (2) 4½" x 5¾" (11.4 x 14.6cm) rectangles
- (6) 3½" x 3½" (8.9 x 8.9cm) squares

FROM FABRIC B (DARK BROWN), CUT:

- (4) Template 1
- (1) Template 15
- (1) Template 9
- (1) Template 9, mirror image
- (1) Template 11
- (1) Template 11, mirror image
- (4) Template 5
- (1) 4½" x 9½" (11.4 x 24.1cm) strip
- (2) 4½" x 13½" (11.4 x 34.3cm) strips

FROM FABRIC C (LIGHT ORANGE), CUT:

- (2) Template 6
- (1) Template 8
- (1) Template 8, mirror image

FROM FABRIC D (DARK ORANGE), CUT:

- (4) Template 4
- (4) 2½" x 2½" (6.4 x 6.4cm) squares

FROM FABRIC E (RED), CUT:

- (3) 3" (7.6cm) x WOF strips, subcut:
  - (16) 3" x 6½" (7.6 x 16.5cm) rectangles
- (11) 1½" (3.8cm) x WOF strips, subcut:
  - (32) 1½" x 5½" (3.8 x 14cm) strips
  - (32) 1½" x 3½" (3.8 x 8.9cm) rectangles
  - (32) 1½" x 2½" (3.8 x 6.4cm) rectangles
  - (32) 1½" x 1½" (3.8 x 3.8cm) squares

FROM FABRIC F (LIGHT GREEN), CUT:

- (1) 4¼" (10.8cm) x WOF strip, subcut:
  - (7) 4¼" x 4¼" (10.8 x 10.8cm) squares
- (2) 3½" (8.9cm) x WOF strips, subcut:
  - (17) 3½" x 3½" (8.9 x 8.9cm) squares
- (1) 2¾" (7cm) x WOF strip, subcut:
  - (10) 2¾" x 2¾" (7 x 7cm) squares
- (8) 2¼" x 2¼" (5.7 x 5.7cm) squares
- (3) 1½" (3.8cm) x WOF strips, subcut:
  - (32) 1½" x 2½" (3.8 x 6.4cm) strips
  - (32) 1½" x 1½" (3.8 x 3.8cm) squares

FROM FABRIC G (DARK GREEN), CUT:

- (1) 4¼" (10.8cm) x WOF strips, subcut:
  - (7) 4¼" x 4¼" (10.8 x 10.8cm) squares
- (2) 3½" (8.9cm) x WOF strips, subcut:
  - (17) 3½" x 3½" (8.9 x 8.9cm) squares
- (1) 2¾" (7cm) x WOF strip, subcut:
  - (10) 2¾" x 2¾" (7 x 7cm) squares
- (8) 2¼" x 2¼" (5.7 x 5.7cm) squares
- (3) 1½" (3.8cm) x WOF strips, subcut:
  - (32) 1½" x 2½" (3.8 x 6.4cm) strips
  - (32) 1½" x 1½" (3.8 x 3.8cm) squares

FROM FABRIC H (BLACK), CUT:

- (2) Template 14
- (2) Template 15
- (2) 1½" (3.8cm) x WOF strips, subcut:
  - (48) 1½" x 1½" (3.8 x 3.8cm) squares

FROM BACKGROUND (CREAM), CUT:

- (2) Template 13
- (2) Template 1
- (6) Template 2
- (1) 15" x 21¼" (38.1 x 54cm) rectangle
- (1) 15" x 17½" (38.1 x 44.5cm) rectangle
- (1) 9" x 21" (22.9 x 53.3cm) strip
- (1) 8¾" x 10½" (22.2 x 26.7cm) rectangle
- (1) 5" x 9½" (12.7 x 24.1cm) strip
- (5) 4½" (11.4cm) x WOF strips, subcut:
  - (2) 4½" x 23" (11.4 x 58.4cm) strips
  - (1) 4½" x 16" (11.4 x 40.6cm) strip
  - (2) 4½" x 9" (11.4 x 22.9cm) strips
  - (4) 4½" x 6½" (11.4 x 16.5cm) rectangles
  - (5) 4½" x 5" (11.4 x 12.7cm) rectangles
  - (2) 4½" x 4½" (11.4 x 11.4cm) squares
- (3) 3½" x 6½" (8.9 x 16.5cm) rectangles
- (5) 3" (7.6cm) x WOF strips, subcut:
  - (7) 3" x 9" (7.6 x 22.9cm) strips
  - (1) 3" x 6½" (7.6 x 16.5cm) strip
  - (32) 3" x 3" (7.6 x 7.6cm) squares
- (7) 2½" (6.4cm) x WOF strips, subcut:
  - (2) 2½" x 40" (6.4 x 101.6cm) strips
  - (1) 2½" x 32" (6.4 x 81.3cm) strip
  - (2) 2½" x 13" (6.4 x 33cm) strips
  - (2) 2½" x 9" (6.4 x 22.9cm) strips
  - (2) 2½" x 8½" (6.4 x 21.6cm) strips
  - (1) 2½" x 8" (6.4 x 20.3cm) strip
  - (2) 2½" x 4½" (6.4 x 11.4cm) rectangles
- (1) 2¼" (5.7cm) x WOF strip, subcut:
  - (16) 2¼" x 2¼" (5.7 x 5.7cm) squares
- (3) 2" x 5" (5.1 x 12.7cm) rectangles
- (8) 1½" (3.8cm) x WOF strips, subcut:
  - (32) 1½" x 2½" (3.8 x 6.4cm) rectangles
  - (138) 1½" x 1½" (3.8 x 3.8cm) squares
  - (2) 1½" x 5" (3.8 x 12.7cm) rectangles
- (2) 1¼" (3.2cm) x WOF strips, subcut:
  - (60) 1¼" x 1¼" (3.2 x 3.2cm) squares

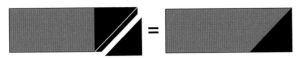

7. Place the marked Fabric H square, RST, on the right side of a 1½" x 3½" (3.8 x 8.9cm) Fabric E rectangle. Sew down the marked line, and trim ¼" (6.4mm) away from the sewn line. Press toward the Fabric H piece. Make (16) units total.

8. Sew (1) 1½" x 3½" (3.8 x 8.9cm) Fabric E rectangle to the right side of all units from step 7. Press toward the Fabric E rectangle.

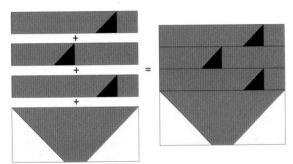

9. Using the units made in steps 3, 6, and 8 and the Assembly Diagram, piece (16) units that are the bottoms of the Strawberry block. Set aside.

10. Mark a diagonal line on the back of (16) 2¼" x 2¼" (5.7 x 5.7cm) Background squares.

11. Pair (8) marked Background squares, RST, with (8) 2¼" x 2¼" (5.7 x 5.7cm) Fabric F squares. Sew ¼" (6.4mm) away from the marked line on both sides.

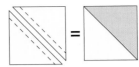

12. Cut down the marked line, and press toward the Fabric F piece. Square the HST to 1½" x 1½" (3.8 x 3.8cm). Make (16) HSTs total.

13. Place (8) marked Background squares, RST, with (8) 2¼" x 2¼" (5.7 x 5.7cm) Fabric G squares. Sew ¼" (6.4mm) away from the marked line on both sides.

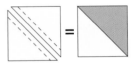

14. Cut down the marked line, and press toward the Fabric G piece. Square the HST to 1½" x 1½" (3.8 x 3.8cm). Make (16) HSTs total.

15. Mark a diagonal line on the back of (96) 1½" x 1½" (3.8 x 3.8cm) Background squares.

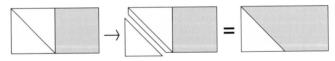

16. Place a marked Background square, RST, on the left side of a 1½" x 2½" (3.8 x 6.4cm) Fabric F rectangle. Sew down the marked line. Trim ¼" (6.4mm) away from the sewn line, and press toward the Background piece. Make (32) units total. Set (16) aside.

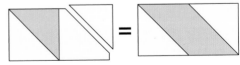

17. Place (1) marked Background square, RST, on the right side of the (16) remaining units. Sew down the marked line. Trim ¼" (6.4mm) away from the sewn line, and press toward the Background piece.

18. Place a marked Background square, RST, on the right side of a 1½" x 2½" (3.8 x 6.4cm) Fabric G rectangle. Sew down the marked line. Trim ¼" (6.4mm) away from the sewn line, and press toward the Background piece. Make (32) units total. Set (16) aside.

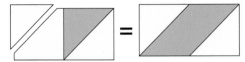

19. Place (1) marked Background square, RST, on the left side of the (16) remaining units. Sew down the marked line. Trim ¼" (6.4mm) away from the sewn line and press toward the Background piece.

20. Mark a diagonal line on the back of (32) 1½" x 1½" (3.8 x 3.8cm) Fabric F squares and (32) 1½" x 1½" (3.8 x 3.8cm) Fabric G squares.

21. Place a marked Fabric F square, RST, on the right side of a 1½" x 2½" (3.8 x 6.4cm) Fabric E strip. Sew down the marked line, then trim ¼" (6.4mm) away from the sewn line. Press toward the Fabric F piece.

22. Place a marked Fabric G square, RST, on the left side of the unit from step 21. Sew down the marked line, then trim ¼" (6.4mm) away from the sewn line. Press toward the Fabric G piece. This creates a Flying Geese block. Make (32) Flying Geese blocks total.

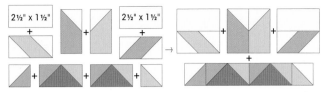

23. Join the units made in steps 12–22 and (2) 1½" x 2½" (3.8 x 6.4cm) rectangles according to the Assembly Diagram. Make (16) units total for the tops of the Strawberry block.

24. Piece together each strawberry top with a strawberry bottom to create a Strawberry block. Press the seam open. Make (16) Strawberry blocks total.

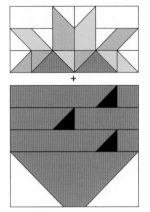

PIECING THE OWL HEAD

25. Sew a Template 5–Fabric B piece to a Template 4–Fabric D piece. Use the curve method of your choice (pages 9–10). Press toward the Template 4 piece. Make (4) units total.

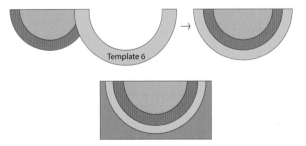

26. Sew a Template 6–Fabric C piece to the unit. Press toward the center. Sew a Template 7–Fabric A piece to the unit. Press toward the center. Make (2) units total.

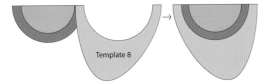

27. Sew a left-facing Template 8–Fabric C piece to a remaining unit completed in step 25. Press toward the center.

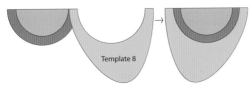

28. Sew a right-facing Template 8–Fabric C piece to a remaining unit completed in step 25. Press toward the center.

29. Sew a left-facing Template 10–Fabric A piece to a right-facing Template 9–Fabric B piece. Press the seam open.

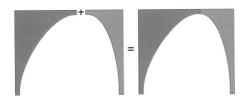

30. Sew a right-facing Template 10–Fabric A piece to a left-facing Template 9–Fabric B piece. Press the seam open.

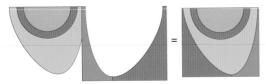

31. Sew the unit from step 30 to the unit from step 27. Press toward the center.

32. Sew the unit from step 29 to the unit from step 28. Press toward the center.

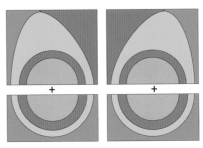

33. Sew a unit from step 31 and 32 to the top of the units from step 26 as shown. Press the seams open. This makes (2) Eye blocks.

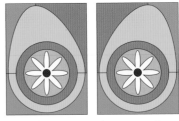

34. Using raw edge appliqué (page 11), apply (1) Template 13–Background piece to each Eye block as shown. Then appliqué the Template 14–Fabric H pieces on top.

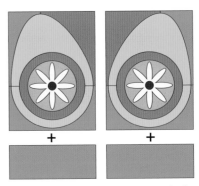

35. Sew (1) 4½" x 10½" (11.4 x 26.7cm) Fabric A strip to the bottom of each Eye block. Press toward the Fabric A pieces.

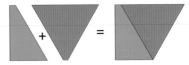

36. Sew a Template 16A–Fabric A piece to the left of a Template 15–Fabric B piece. Press toward the Template 16A piece.

37. Sew a Template 16B–Fabric A piece to the right of the unit. Press toward the Template 16B piece.

38. Sew a Template 16A–Fabric A piece to the left of a Template 15–Fabric H piece. Press toward the Template 16A piece.

39. Sew a Template 16B–Fabric A piece to the right of the unit. Press toward the Template 16B piece. Make (2) units total.

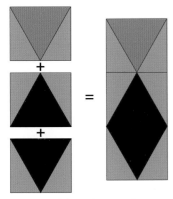

40. Sew together the (3) units as shown. Press the seams open.

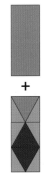

41. Sew a 4½" x 9½" (11.4 x 24.1cm) Fabric B strip to the top of the unit. Press toward the Fabric B piece.

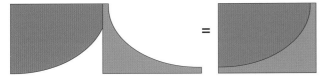

42. Sew a left-facing Template 12–Fabric A piece to a left-facing Template 11–Fabric B piece. Press toward the center.

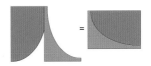

43. Sew a right-facing Template 12–Fabric A piece to a right-facing Template 11–Fabric B piece. Press toward the center.

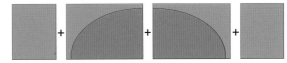

44. Sew the (2) units together, pressing the seam open. Sew a 4½" x 5¾" (11.4 x 14.6cm) Fabric A piece onto both sides of the unit. Press toward the Fabric A pieces.

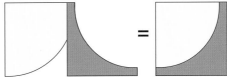

45. Sew a Template 2–Fabric A piece to a Template 1–Background piece. Press toward the center. Square the block to 4½" x 4½" (11.4 x 11.4cm). This will make a Drunkard's Path block. Make (2) Drunkard's Path blocks.

46. Sew the (2) Drunkard's Path blocks onto both sides of (1) 4½" x 16" (11.4 x 40.6cm) Background strip. Press toward the Background strip.

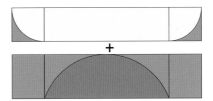

47. Sew the unit from step 44 to the bottom of the unit from step 46. Press the seam open.

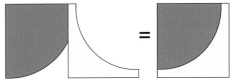

48. Sew a Template 2–Background piece to a Template 1–Fabric B piece. Press toward the center. Square the block to 4½" x 4½" (11.4 x 11.4cm). This will make a Drunkard's Path block. Make (4) Drunkard's Path blocks. Set (2) aside for the Owl Bottom.

49. Sew (1) 4½" x 23" (11.4 x 58.4cm) Background strip to the top of each Drunkard's Path block as shown. Press toward the Background strip.

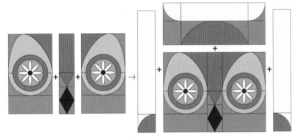

50. Use the diagram to join all the completed units. Press the seams open. This completes the Owl Head block.

PIECING THE OWL BOTTOM

51. Mark a diagonal line on the back of (6) 3½" x 3½" (8.9 x 8.9cm) Fabric A squares. Place a marked Fabric A square, RST, on the left side of a 3½" x 6½" (8.9 x 16.5cm) Background strip. Sew down the marked line. Trim ¼" (6.4mm) away from the sewn line and press toward the Fabric A piece.

52. Place a marked Fabric A square, RST, on the right side of the unit. Sew down the marked line. Trim ¼" (6.4mm) away from the sewn line, and press toward the Fabric A piece. This creates a Flying Geese block. Make (3) Flying Geese blocks total.

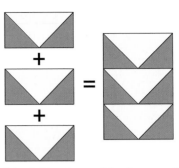

53. Sew the (3) Flying Geese blocks together as shown. Press the seams open.

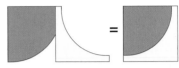

54. Sew a Template 2–Background piece to a Template 1–Fabric A piece. Press toward the center. Square the block to 4½" x 4½" (11.4 x 11.4cm). This will make a Drunkard's Path block. Make (2) Drunkard's Path blocks total.

55. Join the (2) Drunkard's Path blocks to both sides of (1) 4½" x 16½" (11.4 x 41.9cm) Fabric A strip as shown. Press toward the Fabric A strip.

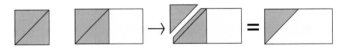

56. Mark a diagonal line on the back of (4) 2½" x 2½" (6.4 x 6.4cm) Fabric D squares. Place a marked Fabric D square, RST, on the left side of a 2½" x 4½" (6.4 x 11.4cm) Background strip. Sew down the marked line. Trim ¼" (6.4mm) away from the sewn line and press toward the Fabric D piece.

57. Place a marked Fabric D square, RST, on the right side of the unit. Sew down the marked line. Trim ¼" (6.4mm) away from the sewn line, and press toward the Fabric D piece, creating a Flying Geese block. Make (2) Flying Geese blocks total.

58. Sew a 2½" x 8½" (6.4 x 21.6cm) Background strip to the left of a Fabric D Flying Geese block. Sew a 2½" x 8½" (6.4 x 21.6cm) Background strip to the right of the other Fabric D Flying Geese block. Press toward the Background strips.

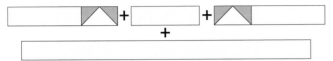

59. Join the (2) units to both sides of (1) 2½" x 8" (6.4 x 20.3cm) Background strip as shown. Then sew a 2½" x 32" (6.4 x 81.3cm) Background strip to the bottom of the unit. Press toward the Background strips.

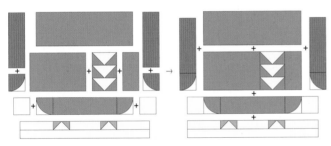

60. Use the diagram to assemble the Owl Bottom block.

PIECING THE LEAF BLOCK

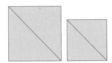

61. Mark a diagonal line on the back of (7) 4¼" x 4¼" (10.8 x 10.8cm) Fabric F squares and (10) 3½" x 3½" (8.9 x 8.9cm) Fabric F squares.

62. Place a 4¼" x 4¼" (10.8 x 10.8cm) Fabric F square, RST, with a 4¼" x 4¼" (10.8 x 10.8cm) Fabric G square. Place a 3½" x 3½" (8.9 x 8.9cm) Fabric F square, RST, with a 3½" x 3½" (8.9 x 8.9cm) Fabric G square. Sew ¼" (6.4mm) away from the sewn line on both sides of each block.

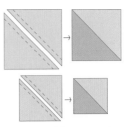

63. Cut down the marked line, and press toward the Fabric G piece. Square the 4¼" x 4¼" (10.8 x 10.8cm) HST to 3½" x 3½" (8.9 x 8.9cm). Make (14) large HSTs total. Square the 3½" x 3½" (8.9 x 8.9cm) HST to 2¾" x 2¾" (7 x 7cm). Make (20) small HSTs.

64. Mark a diagonal line on the back of (42) 1½" x 1½" (3.8 x 3.8cm) Background squares and (60) 1¼" x 1¼" (3.2 x 3.2cm) Background squares.

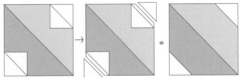

65. Place (2) marked 1½" x 1½" (3.8 x 3.8cm) squares, RST, in opposing corners of a large HST as shown. Sew down the marked lines. Trim ¼" (6.4mm) away from the sewn lines and press toward the Background pieces. Make (7) units total.

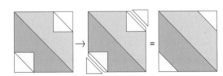

66. Place (2) marked 1¼" x 1¼" (3.2 x 3.2cm) squares, RST, in opposing corners of a small HST as shown. Sew down the marked lines. Trim ¼" (6.4mm) away from the sewn lines and press toward the Background pieces. Make (10) units total.

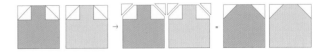

67. Place (2) marked 1½" x 1½" (3.8 x 3.8cm) squares, RST, in adjacent corners of (1) 3½" x 3½" (8.9 x 8.9cm) Fabric F square and (1) 3½" x 3½" (8.9 x 8.9cm) Fabric G square as shown. Sew down the marked lines. Trim ¼" (6.4mm) away from the sewn lines, and press toward the Background pieces. Make (7) units of each color.

68. Place (2) marked 1¼" x 1¼" (3.2 x 3.2cm) squares, RST, in adjacent corners of (1) 2¾" x 2¾" (7 x 7cm) Fabric F square and (1) 2¾" x 2¾" (7 x 7cm) Fabric G square as shown. Sew down the marked lines. Trim ¼" (6.4mm) away from the sewn lines, and press toward the Background pieces. Make (10) units of each color.

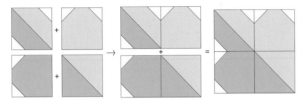

69. Use the diagram to assemble (1) of each unit into a Leaf block as shown. Be sure to use the same-sized units for two different Leaf blocks. Make (7) large Leaf blocks and (10) small Leaf blocks total.

QUILT TOP ASSEMBLY

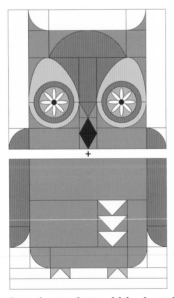

70. Sew together the Owl Head block and the Owl Bottom block as shown.

71. Sew together (1) 2½" x 40" (6.4 x 101.6cm) Background strip to (1) 2½" x 13" (6.4 x 33cm) Background strip, creating a 2½" x 52½" (6.4 x 133.4cm) strip. Make (2) strips total. Sew the strips to the sides of the Owl block. Press toward the Background strips.

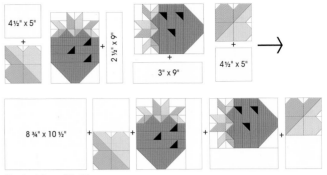

Section1 Assembly Diagram

72. Use the Section 1 Assembly Diagram to assemble the first strawberry section of the quilt top.

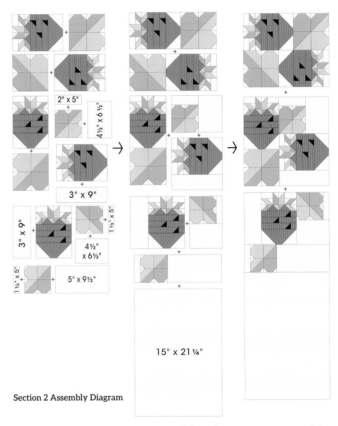

Section 2 Assembly Diagram

73. Use the Section 2 Assembly Diagram to assemble the second strawberry section of the quilt top.

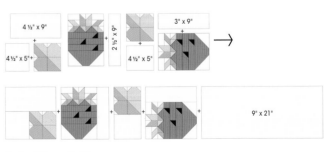

Section 3 Assembly Diagram

74. Use the Section 3 Assembly Diagram to assemble the third strawberry section of the quilt top.

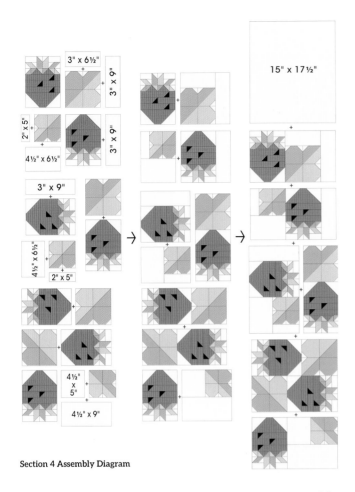

Section 4 Assembly Diagram

75. Use the Section 4 Assembly Diagram to assemble the fourth strawberry section of the quilt top.

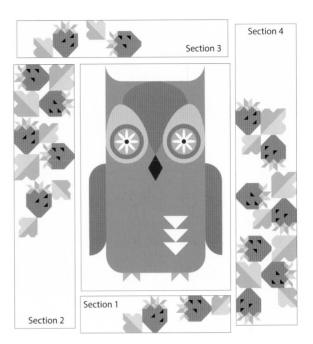

76. Use the Quilt Top Assembly Diagram to sew together the Owl block with Sections 1–4 to complete the quilt top. The sections are pieced to the Owl block in their numeric order.

FINISHING

77. Make a three-layer quilt sandwich. Make sure the backing piece is at least 2" (5.1cm) larger all the way around the quilt top. Quilt and bind as desired.

Finished Size: 56½" x 56½" (1.4 x 1.4m)

Skill Level: Intermediate

Fabrics Used: Art Gallery Fabrics Icy Mint, Parisian Blue, Burnt Orange, and Crystal Pink

Pieced by Kelly Stauffer

Longarmed by Erin Grogan

SO MOD QUILT

So Mod, like Retro Blooms, was inspired by the mid-century modern aesthetic. The sleek, simple curves create a very clean and sophisticated look. The gentle curves in this design make for an easy chain-piecing pattern that comes together quickly.

MATERIALS

Yardage is based on 42" (1.1m) wide fabric. Backing assumes at least 4" (10.2cm) coverage on all sides.

So Mod Templates (page 153)

1½ yards (1.4m) in Fabric A (Mint)

1½ yards (1.4m) in Fabric B (Blue)

1¼ yards (1.1m) in Fabric C (Orange)

1 yard (91.4cm) in Fabric D (Pink)

3⅝ yards (3.3m) in backing fabric

½ yard (45.7cm) in binding fabric

67" x 67" (1.7 x 1.7m) in batting

CUTTING

All templates include a ¼" (6.4mm) seam allowance. Mirror image of a template means to turn the template upside down so that the template text is right side touching the fabric.

FROM FABRIC A (MINT), CUT:

(16) Template 1

(8) Template 2

(8) Template 2, mirror image

(8) Template 3

(8) Template 3, mirror image

FROM FABRIC B (BLUE), CUT:

(16) Template 1

(8) Template 2

(8) Template 2, mirror image

(8) Template 3

(8) Template 3, mirror image

FROM FABRIC C (ORANGE), CUT:

(16) Template 1

(16) Template 2

(16) Template 2, mirror image

(8) Template 3

(8) Template 3, mirror image

FROM FABRIC D (PINK), CUT:

(16) Template 1

(8) Template 3

(8) Template 3, mirror image

PIECING BLOCK 1

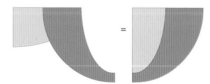
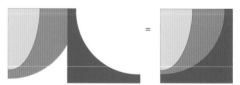

1. Place a Template 3–Fabric D piece, RST, with a left-facing Template 2–Fabric C piece as shown. Line up the template ends and sew the pieces together, working slowly around the curve. Use the curve method of your choice (pages 9–10). Press the seam toward Template 2.

2. Place a left-facing Template 1–Fabric B, RST, with the unit as shown. Line up the template ends and sew the pieces together, working slowly around the curve. Press the seam toward Template 1. Starch and press the block.

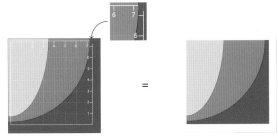

3. Line the ruler up ¼" (6.4mm) from the top-right seam line between Template 1 and Template 2 as shown. Trim off the excess from the right side of the block.

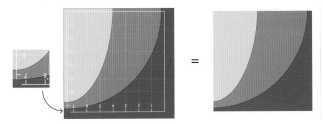

4. Line the ruler up with the bottom-left seam line between Template 1 and Template 2 as shown. Trim off the excess from the bottom of the block.

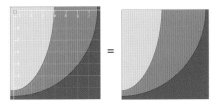

5. Line the ruler up with the block's bottom-right corner, and trim the excess from the top and left of the block as shown. This squares Block 1 to 7½" x 7½" (19.1 x 19.1cm). Make (2) Block 1s total.

PIECING BLOCK 2

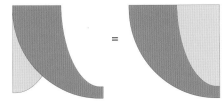

6. Place a Template 3–Fabric D piece, RST, with a right-facing Template 2–Fabric C piece as shown. Line up the template ends and sew the pieces together, working slowly around the curve. Press the seam toward Template 2.

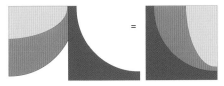

7. Place a right-facing Template 1–Fabric B, RST, with the unit as shown. Line up the template ends and sew the pieces together, working slowly around the curve. Press the seam toward Template 1. Starch and press the block.

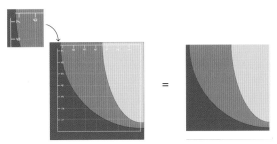

8. Line the ruler up ¼" (6.4mm) from the top-left seam line between Template 1 and Template 2 as shown. Trim off the excess from the left side of the block.

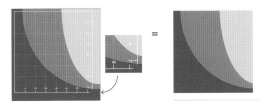

9. Line the ruler up with the bottom-right seam line between Template 1 and Template 2 as shown. Trim off the excess from the bottom of the block.

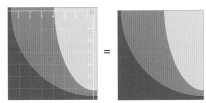

10. Line the ruler up with the block's bottom-left corner, and trim the excess from the top and right of the block as shown. This squares Block 2 to 7½" x 7½" (19.1 x 19.1cm). Make (2) Block 2s total.

PIECING THE CIRCLE BLOCK

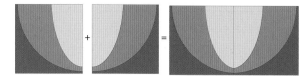

11. Pair a Block 1 with a Block 2 and sew them together as shown. Make (2) units total.

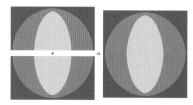

12. Sew the (2) units together as shown. Press the seam open. This completes the Circle Block. The Circle Block finishes at 14½" x 14½" (36.8 x 36.8cm).

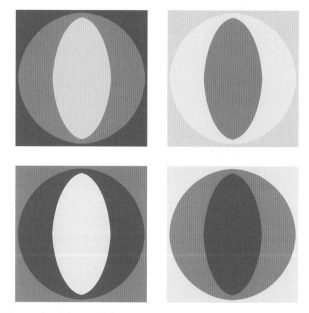

13. Make (4) Circle Blocks in each of the four colorways.

QUILT TOP ASSEMBLY

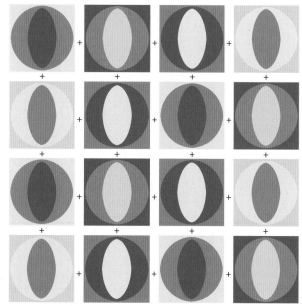

14. Use the diagram to assemble the quilt top rows. Press the seams open. Sew the (4) rows together to complete the top. Press the seams open.

FINISHING

15. Make a three-layer quilt sandwich. Make sure the backing piece is at least 2" (5.1cm) larger all the way around the quilt top. Quilt and bind as desired.

Finished Size: 54" x 65" (1.4 x 1.7m)

Skill Level: Intermediate

Fabrics Use: Art Gallery Fabrics Pure Solids Desert Dunes, Turmeric, Mirage Blue, and White Linen

Pieced & Quilted by Erin Grogan

RETRO STARS QUILT

Following World War II was the great Space Race between the United States and the Soviet Union. With this came the atomic era, marked by the rising fear of nuclear power and fascination with space exploration, scientific discovery, and futurism. Retro Stars tells the story of this era's love for space by using Sawtooth Star blocks. The interlocking, curving motifs are a nod to atomic design and are reminiscent of retro televisions.

MATERIALS

Yardage is based on 42" (1.1m) wide fabric. Backing assumes at least 4" (10.2cm) coverage on all sides.

Retro Stars Templates (page 154)

½ yard (45.7cm) in Fabric A (Red)

¾ yard (68.6cm) in Fabric B (Yellow)

½ yard (45.7cm) in Fabric C (Blue)

3 yards (2.7m) in Background (Cream)

4 yards (3.7m) in backing fabric

½ yard (45.7cm) in binding fabric

64" x 75" (1.6 x 1.9m) in batting

PIECING THE SMALL SAWTOOTH STAR BLOCK

1. Mark a diagonal line on the back of (56) 1½" x 1½" (3.8 x 3.8cm) Fabric A squares and (48) 1½" x 1½" (3.8 x 3.8cm) Fabric C squares.

 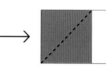

2. Place a marked Fabric A square, RST, on the left side of a 1½" x 2½" (3.8 x 6.4cm) Background piece. Sew down the marked line.

3. Trim ¼" (6.4mm) away from the sewn line, and press toward the Fabric A piece.

4. Place a marked Fabric A square, RST, on the right side of the unit. Sew down the marked line.

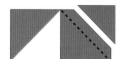 

5. Trim ¼" (6.4mm) away from the sewn line, and press toward the Fabric A piece. This completes a Flying Geese block. Make (28) Fabric A Flying Geese total.

6. Repeat steps 2–5 with the (48) marked Fabric C squares. Make (24) Fabric C Flying Geese total.

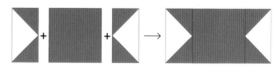

7. Sew (2) Fabric A Flying Geese blocks to the sides of (1) 2½" x 2½" (6.4 x 6.4cm) Fabric A square. Press toward the square. Make (7) units total.

8. Sew (2) 1½" x 1½" (3.8 x 3.8cm) Background squares to the sides of (14) Fabric A Flying Geese. Press toward the Background pieces.

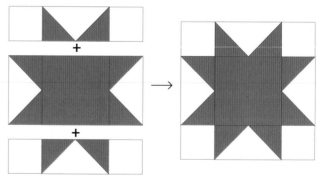

9. Sew (2) units from step 8 to the top and bottom of (1) unit from step 7. Press the seams open. This completes a small Sawtooth Star block. Make (7) Fabric A Sawtooth Star blocks total.

CUTTING

All templates include a ¼" (6.4mm) seam allowance.

FROM FABRIC A (RED), CUT:

- (2) 2½" (6.4cm) x WOF strips, subcut:
  - (1) 2½" x 15" (6.4 x 38.1cm) strip
  - (1) 2½" x 9½" (6.4 x 24.1cm) strip
  - (1) 2½" x 7½" (6.4 x 19.1cm) strip
  - (1) 2½" x 6½" (6.4 x 16.5cm) strip
  - (1) 2½" x 5½" (6.4 x 14cm) strip
  - (2) 2½" x 3½" (6.4 x 8.9cm) rectangles
  - (7) 2½" x 2½" (6.4 x 6.4cm) squares
- (2) 1½" (3.8cm) x WOF strips, subcut:
  - (56) 1½" x 1½" (3.8 x 3.8cm) squares
- (1) 3½" x 6½" (8.9 x 16.5cm) rectangle
- (1) 5½" x 6½" (14 x 16.5cm) rectangle
- (2) Template 1
- (2) Template 4
- (2) Template 6
- (2) Template 7

FROM FABRIC B (YELLOW), CUT:

- (1) 4½" (11.4cm) x WOF strip, subcut:
  - (1) 4½" x 8½" (11.4 x 21.6cm) strip
  - (1) 4½" x 7½" (11.4 x 19.1cm) strip
  - (5) 4½" x 4½" (11.4 x 11.4cm) squares
- (5) 2½" (6.4cm) x WOF strips, subcut:
  - (1) 2½" x 13½" (6.4 x 34.3cm) strip
  - (1) 2½" x 12½" (6.4 x 31.8cm) strip
  - (7) 2½" x 6½" (6.4 x 16.5cm) strips
  - (1) 2½" x 4½" (6.4 x 11.4cm) rectangle
  - (2) 2½" x 3½" (6.4 x 8.9cm) rectangles
  - (40) 2½" x 2½" (6.4 x 6.4cm) squares
- (4) Template 1
- (8) Template 4
- (4) Template 5

FROM FABRIC C (BLUE), CUT:

- (1) 8½" x 8½" (21.6 x 21.6cm) square
- (1) 6½" x 10½" (16.5 x 26.7cm) rectangle
- (1) 3½" x 3½" (8.9 x 8.9cm) square
- (2) 2½" (6.4cm) x WOF strips, subcut:
  - (3) 2½" x 8½" (6.4 x 21.6cm) strips
  - (1) 2½" x 6½" (6.4 x 16.5cm) strip
  - (1) 2½" x 4½" (6.4 x 11.4cm) rectangle
  - (6) 2½" x 2½" (6.4 x 6.4cm) squares
- (3) 1½" (3.8cm) x WOF strips, subcut:
  - (1) 1½" x 6½" (3.8 x 16.5cm) strip
  - (48) 1½" x 1½" (3.8 x 3.8cm) squares
- (4) Template 1
- (5) Template 2
- (1) Template 3

FROM BACKGROUND (WHITE), CUT:

- (1) 8½" x 8½" (21.6 x 21.6cm) square
- (1) 7½" x 11½" (19.1 x 29.2cm) rectangle
- (1) 6½" (16.5cm) x WOF strip, subcut:
  - (1) 6½" x 10½" (16.5 x 26.7cm) rectangle
  - (1) 6½" x 12½" (16.5 x 31.8cm) strips
  - (1) 6½" x 6½" (16.5 x 16.5cm) square
- (2) 5½" x 9½" (14 x 24.1cm) rectangles
- (10) 4½" (11.4cm) x WOF strips, subcut:
  - (2) 4½" x 34½" (11.4 x 87.6cm) strips
  - (1) 4½" x 31½" (11.4 x 80cm) strip
  - (2) 4½" x 30½" (11.4 x 77.5cm) strips
  - (2) 4½" x 18½" (11.4 x 47cm) strips
  - (3) 4½" x 12½" (11.4 x 31.8cm) strips
  - (1) 4½" x 9½" (11.4 x 24.1cm) strip
  - (9) 4½" x 8½" (11.4 x 21.6cm) strips
  - (1) 4½" x 6½" (11.4 x 16.5cm) rectangle
  - (8) 4½" x 4½" (11.4 x 11.4cm) square
- (2) 3½" (8.9cm) x WOF strips, subcut:
  - (1) 3½" x 7½" (8.9 x 19.1cm) strip
  - (2) 3½" x 6½" (8.9 x 16.5cm) rectangles
  - (2) 3½" x 4½" (8.9 x 11.4cm) rectangles
  - (4) 3½" x 3½" (8.9 x 8.9cm) squares
  - (1) 3½" x 1½" (8.9 x 3.8cm) rectangle
- (6) 2½" (6.4cm) x WOF strips, subcut:
  - (1) 2½" x 20½" (6.4 x 52.1cm) strip
  - (2) 2½" x 16½" (6.4 x 41.9cm) strips
  - (2) 2½" x 6½" (6.4 x 16.5cm) strips
  - (24) 2½" x 4½" (6.4 x 11.4cm) rectangles
  - (20) 2½" x 2½" (6.4 x 6.4cm) squares
- (6) 1½" (3.8cm) x WOF strips, subcut:
  - (52) 1½" x 2½" (3.8 x 6.4cm) rectangles
  - (52) 1½" x 1½" (3.8 x 3.8cm) squares
- (4) Template 1
- (9) Template 2
- (9) Template 3
- (2) Template 5
- (4) Template 6
- (2) Template 8

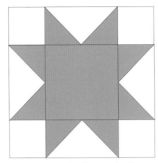

10. Repeat steps 7–9 with the Fabric C Flying Geese and the 2½" x 2½" (6.4 x 6.4cm) Fabric C squares. Make (6) Fabric C Sawtooth Star blocks total.

PIECING THE LARGE SAWTOOTH STAR BLOCK

11. Mark a diagonal line on the back of (40) 2½" x 2½" (6.4 x 6.4cm) Fabric B squares.

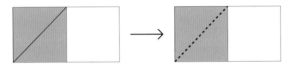

12. Place a marked Fabric B square, RST, on the left side of a 2½" x 4½" (6.4 x 11.4cm) Background piece. Sew down the marked line.

13. Trim ¼" (6.4mm) away from the sewn line, and press toward the Fabric B piece.

14. Place a marked Fabric B square, RST, on the right side of the unit. Sew down the marked line.

15. Trim ¼" (6.4mm) away from the sewn line, and press toward the Fabric B piece. This completes a Flying Geese block. Make (20) Fabric B Flying Geese.

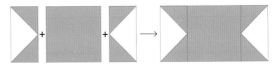

16. Sew (2) Fabric B Flying Geese blocks to the sides of (1) 4½" x 4½" (11.4 x 11.4cm) Fabric B square. Press toward the square. Make (5) units total.

17. Sew (2) 2½" x 2½" (6.4 x 6.4cm) Background squares to the sides of (10) Fabric B Flying Geese. Press toward the Background pieces.

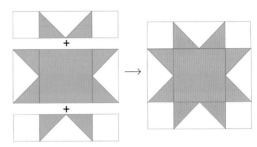

18. Sew (2) units from step 17 to the top and bottom of (1) unit from step 16. Press the seams open. This completes a large Sawtooth Star block. Make (5) Fabric B Sawtooth Star blocks total.

PIECING THE DRUNKARD'S PATH BLOCK

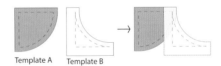

Template A   Template B

19. Place a Template A piece, RST, with a Template B piece as shown. Pay attention to the template numbers in the chart.

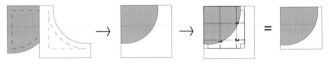

20. Sew the pieces together, gently nesting the Template B piece into the curve of the Template A piece. Use the curve method of your choice (pages 9–10). Press toward the Template B piece. Lining up your ruler's ¼" (6.4mm) marks along the pieced seam, square the block to the size provided in the Drunkard's Path Chart. Make the quantity of blocks indicated.

DRUNKARD'S PATH CHART

Label		Template A	Template B	Square-Up Size	Qty
#1 DP		Template 1–Fabric C	Template 2–Background	2½" x 2½" (6.4 x 6.4cm)	4
#2 DP		Template 1–Background	Template 2–Fabric C	2½" x 2½" (6.4 x 6.4cm)	4
#3 DP		Template 1–Fabric B	Template 2–Background	2½" x 2½" (6.4 x 6.4cm)	3
#4 DP		Template 1–Fabric B	Template 2–Fabric C	2½" x 2½" (6.4 x 6.4cm)	1
#5 DP		Template 1–Fabric A	Template 2–Background	2½" x 2½" (6.4 x 6.4cm)	2
#6 DP		Template 3–Background	Template 4–Fabric B	3½" x 3½" (8.9 x 8.9cm)	7
#7 DP		Template 3–Fabric C	Template 4–Fabric B	3½" x 3½" (8.9 x 8.9cm)	1
#8 DP		Template 3–Background	Template 4–Fabric A	3½" x 3½" (8.9 x 8.9cm)	2
#9 DP		Template 5–Fabric B	Template 6–Background	4½" x 4½" (11.4 x 11.4cm)	4
#10 DP		Template 5–Background	Template 6–Fabric A	4½" x 4½" (11.4 x 11.4cm)	2
#11 DP		Template 7–Fabric A	Template 8–Background	6½" x 6½" (16.5 x 16.5cm)	2

SECTION 1 ASSEMBLY

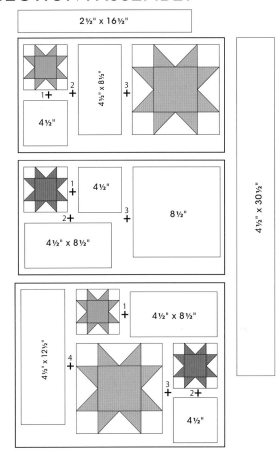

21. Use the diagram to piece the first section of the quilt. The pieces of each section are joined in the numeric order shown. Press the seams open.

SECTION 2 ASSEMBLY

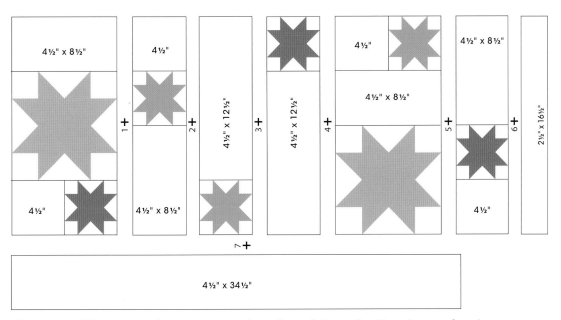

22. Use the diagram to piece the second section of the quilt. The pieces of each section are joined in the numeric order shown. Press the seams open.

SECTION 3 ASSEMBLY

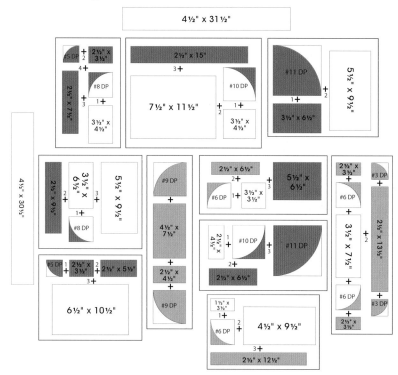

23. Use the diagram to piece the third section of the quilt. The pieces of each section are joined in the numeric order shown. Press the seams open.

SECTION 4 ASSEMBLY

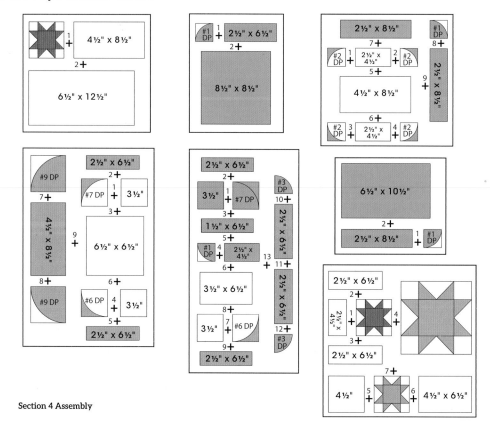

Section 4 Assembly

Section 4 Assembly

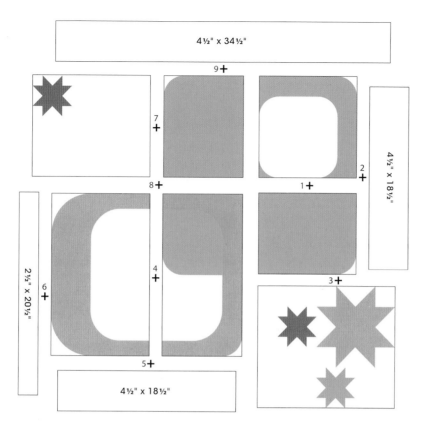

24. Use the diagrams to piece the fourth section of the quilt. The pieces of each section are joined in the numeric order shown. Press the seams open.

QUILT TOP ASSEMBLY

25. Sew Section 1 to the right of Section 3, and press the seam open. Sew Section 4 to the right of Section 2, and press the seam open.

26. Join the (2) sections together as shown, and press the seam open.

FINISHING

27. Make a three-layer quilt sandwich. Make sure the backing piece is at least 2" (5.1cm) larger all the way around the quilt top. Quilt and bind as desired.

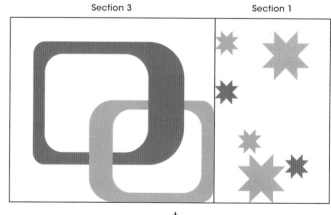

Section 3   Section 1

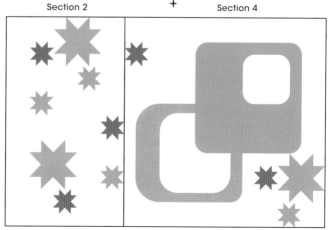

Section 2   +   Section 4

Finished size: 20" x 29" (50.8 x 73.7cm)

Skill Level: Intermediate

Fabrics Used: Art Gallery Fabrics Pure Solids Tigerlily, Desert Dunes, Sweet Tangerine, Turmeric, Mirage Blue, Wisteria, Parisian Blue, Heart of the Ocean, and Snow

Pieced & Quilted by Erin Grogan

SETTING SUN WALL HANGING

As we transition out of the '60s and into the '70s, the hippie era faded into a celebration of individualism, the introduction of disco, and a new generation of surfers. Surfing was no longer viewed as only a hobby, but some surfers did become professional "beach bums." The Setting Sun Wall Hanging celebrates the beauty of being one with the ocean.

MATERIALS

Yardage is based on 42" (1.1m) wide fabric. Backing assumes at least 4" (10.2cm) coverage on all sides.

Setting Sun Templates (page 155)

1 Fat Eighth in Fabric A (Red)

1 Fat Eighth in Fabric B (Dark Red)

1 Fat Quarter in Fabric C (Orange)

½ yard (45.7cm) in Fabric D (Yellow)

⅛ yard (11.4cm) in Fabric E (Teal)

⅛ yard (11.4cm) in Fabric F (Purple)

⅛ yard (11.4cm) in Fabric G (Light Blue)

⅛ yard (11.4cm) in Fabric H (Dark Blue)

½ yard (45.7cm) in Background (Cream)

1 yard (91.4cm) in backing fabric

¼ yard (22.9cm) in binding fabric

26" x 36" (66 x 91.4cm) in batting

CUTTING

All templates include a ¼" (6.4mm) seam allowance.

FROM FABRIC A (RED), CUT:

(4) Template 1

FROM FABRIC B (DARK RED), CUT:

(4) Template 2

FROM FABRIC C (ORANGE), CUT:

(4) Template 3

FROM FABRIC D (YELLOW), CUT:

(4) Template 4

FROM FABRIC E (TEAL), CUT:

(1) 1½" x 20" (3.8 x 50.8cm)

FROM FABRIC F (PURPLE), CUT:

(1) 2½" x 20" (6.4 x 50.8cm)

FROM FABRIC G (LIGHT BLUE), CUT:

(1) 3½" x 20" (8.9 x 50.8cm)

FROM FABRIC H (DARK BLUE), CUT:

(1) 4½" x 20" (11.4 x 50.8cm)

FROM BACKGROUND (WHITE), CUT:

(4) Template 5

(2) 3" x 14½" (7.6 x 36.8cm)

(5) 1½" x 20" (3.8 x 50.8cm)

PIECING THE SUN BLOCK

1. Place a Template 1–Fabric A piece, RST, with a Template 2–Fabric B piece. Sew them together as shown, gently lining up the raw edge of the Template 2 piece with the raw edge of the Template 1 piece. Use the curve method of your choice (pages 9 -10). Press toward the Template 2 piece.

2. Place a Template 3–Fabric C piece, RST, with the unit. Sew them together as shown, gently lining up the raw edge of the Template 3 piece with the raw edge of the Template 2 piece. Press toward the Template 3 piece.

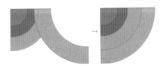

3. Place a Template 4–Fabric D piece, RST, with the unit. Sew them together as shown, gently lining up the raw edge of the Template 4 piece with the raw edge of the Template 3 piece. Press toward the Template 4 piece.

4. Place a Template 5–Background piece, RST, with the unit. Sew the pieces together, gently nesting the Template 5 piece into the curve of the unit. Press toward the Template 5 piece.

5. Square the Drunkard's Path block to 7½" x 7½" (19.1 x 19.1cm). Make (4) Drunkard's Path blocks total.

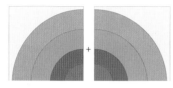

6. Sew (2) Drunkard's Path blocks together as shown, lining up the seams. Press the seams open. Make (2) units total.

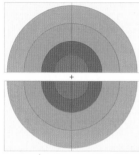

7. Sew the (2) units together as shown. Press the seam open.

WALL HANGING ASSEMBLY

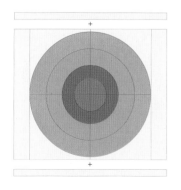

8. Sew (2) 3" x 14½" (7.6 x 36.8cm) Background strips to the sides of the Sun block. Press toward the Background strips.

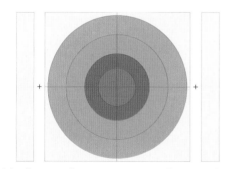

9. Sew a 1½" x 20" (3.8 x 50.8cm) Background strip to the top and bottom of the block. Press toward the Background strips.

10. Referring to the diagram, join the remaining (3) 1½" x 20" (3.8 x 50.8cm) Background strips, (1) 1½" x 20" (3.8 x 50.8cm) Fabric E strip, (1) 2½" x 20" (6.4 x 50.8cm) Fabric F strip, (1) 3½" x 20" (8.9 x 50.8cm) Fabric G strip, and (1) 4½" x 20" (11.4 x 50.8cm) Fabric H strip. Press the seams to the dark side. This creates the bottom of the quilt top.

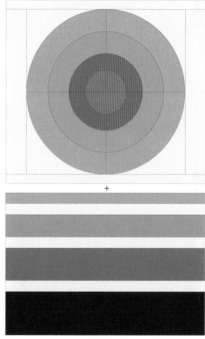

11. Sew the two halves of the wall hanging together as shown. Press toward the dark side.

FINISHING

12. Make a three-layer quilt sandwich. Make sure the backing piece is at least 2" (5.1cm) larger all the way around the wall hanging top. Quilt and bind as desired.

Finished Size: 19" x 27½" (48.3 x 69.9cm)

Skill Level: Intermediate

Fabrics Use: Art Gallery Fabrics Pure Solids Turmeric, Sweet Tangerine, Dessert Dunes, Asparagus, and Creme de la Creme

Pieced & Quilted by Erin Grogan

SPROUT WALL HANGING

Sprout is a small wall hanging that grew from the Retro Blooms Quilt. This little Sprout celebrates the late 1960s and early 1970s wave of "flower power." Hippies used the flower as a means of peaceful protest. They became known as flower children and could be seen with flowers braided into their hair and distributing flowers in public as a promotion of world peace.

MATERIALS

Yardage is based on 42" (1.1m) wide fabric. Backing assumes at least 4" (10.2cm) coverage on all sides.

Retro Blooms Templates (pages 148)

1 Fat Quarter in Fabric A (Yellow)

1 Fat Quarter in Fabric B (Orange)

1 Fat Quarter in Fabric C (Red)

½ yard (45.7cm) in Fabric D (Green)

½ yard (45.7cm) in Background (Cream)

1 yard (91.4cm) in backing fabric

¼ yard (22.9cm) in binding fabric

26" x 36" (66 x 91.4cm) in batting

CUTTING

All templates include a ¼" (6.4mm) seam allowance.

FROM FABRIC A (YELLOW), CUT:

(2) Template 2

(2) 3" x 8" (7.6 x 20.3cm)

FROM FABRIC B (ORANGE), CUT:

(2) Template 3

(2) 2½" x 8" (6.4 x 20.3cm)

FROM FABRIC C (RED), CUT:

(2) Template 4

(2) 3½" x 8" (8.9 x 20.3cm)

FROM FABRIC D (GREEN), CUT:

(6) Template 5

(1) 1" x 14½" (2.5 x 36.8cm)

FROM BACKGROUND (CREAM), CUT:

(8) Template 1

(4) Template 6

(2) 3" x 27½" (7.6 x 69.9cm)

PIECING BLOCK 1

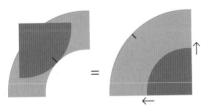
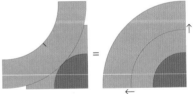

1. Fold a Template 4–Fabric C and Template 3–Fabric B pieces in half. Mark their centers. Place the template pieces, RST, and pin them together at their marked centers. Line up the template ends and sew the pieces together, working slowly around the curve. Use the curve method of your choice (pages 9–10). Press the seam toward Template 3.

2. Fold the unit in half, and mark the center along the Template 3 edge. Fold the Template 2–Fabric A piece in half, and mark the center. Line up the Template 2 piece, RST, with the unit at their centers and pin. Line up the ends of the pieces and sew together. Press the seam toward Template 2.

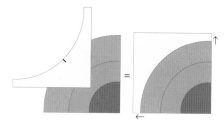

3. Fold a Template 1–Background piece in half, and mark the center. Place the Template 1 piece, RST, with the unit, lining up at their centers. Pin together and sew. Press the seam toward the Template 1 piece.

4. Square the block to 7½" x 7½" (19.1 x 19.1cm). This is Block 1. Make (2) Block 1s total.

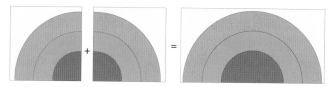

5. With the blocks RST, line up the seams and sew them together as shown. Press the seams open. This will yield (1) unit total.

PIECING BLOCK 2

6. Sew together (1) 3½" x 8" (8.9 x 20.3cm) Fabric C strip, (1) 2½" x 8" (6.4 x 20.3cm) Fabric B strip, and (1) 3" x 8" (7.6 x 20.3cm) Fabric A strip as shown. Press the seams open. Make (2) strip sets total.

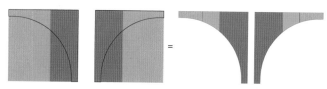

7. Subcut (1) left-facing and (1) right-facing Template 6s from the strip sets as shown. Pay close attention to the template and fabric orientation.

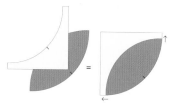

8. Fold a Template 1–Background in half, and mark the center. Fold a Template 5–Fabric D piece in half, marking the center on both sides. Place the Template 1 piece, RST, with the Template 5 piece, lining up at their marked centers on one side. Pin together and sew. Press toward the Template 1 piece.

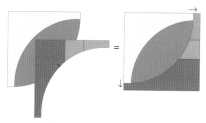

9. Fold a Template 6–strip set piece in half, and mark the center as shown. Place the Template 6 piece, RST, with the unit, lining up at their centers. Pin together and sew. Press toward the Template 6 unit.

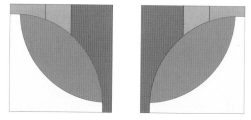

10. Square the block to 7½" x 7½" (19.1 x 19.1cm). This is Block 2. Make (2) Block 2s total.

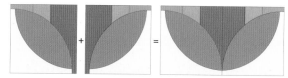

11. With the blocks RST, line up the seams and sew them together as shown. Press the seams open. This will yield (1) unit total.

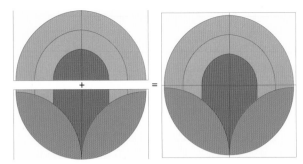

12. Sew together the unit from step 5 with the unit from step 11 as shown. Press the seams open. This completes the Bloom block.

PIECING BLOCK 3

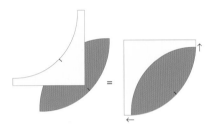

13. Fold a Template 1– Background in half, and mark the center. Fold a Template 5–Fabric D piece in half, marking the center on both sides. Place the Template 1 piece, RST, with the Template 5 piece, lining up at their marked centers on one side. Pin together and sew. Press toward the Template 1 piece.

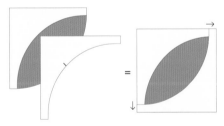

14. Fold a Template 6–Background piece in half, and mark the center as shown. Place the Template 6 piece, RST, with the unit, lining up at their centers. Pin together and sew. Press toward the Template 6 unit.

15. Square the block to 7½" x 7½" (19.1 x 19.1cm). This is Block 3. Make (4) Block 3s total.

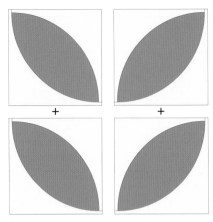

16. Pair (2) Block 3s together as shown. Sew together.

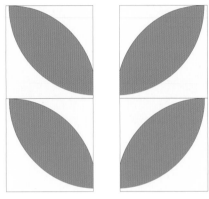

17. Trim ¼" (6.4mm) from the Background edge as shown.

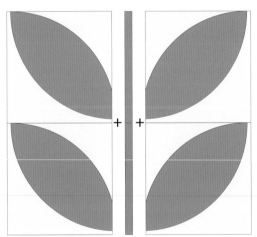

18. Join the (2) units by sewing (1) 1" x 14½" (2.5 x 36.8cm) Fabric D strip between them. Press toward the Fabric D strip. This will yield (1) unit total.

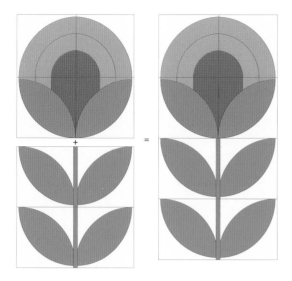

19. Sew the unit to the bottom of the Bloom block completed in step 12. Press the seam open.

WALL HANGING ASSEMBLY

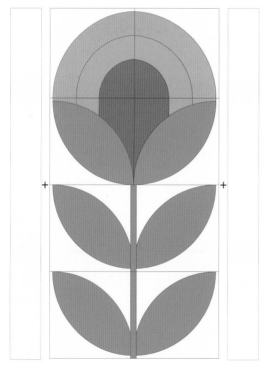

20. Sew (2) 3" x 27½" (7.6 x 69.9cm) Background strips to the sides of the block. Press toward the Background strips, completing the wall hanging.

FINISHING

21. Make a three-layer quilt sandwich. Make sure the backing piece is at least 2" (5.1cm) larger all the way around the wall hanging top. Quilt and bind as desired.

Finished Size: 20" x 20" (50.8 x 50.8cm)

Skill Level: Intermediate

Fabrics Used: Art Gallery Fabrics Pure Solids Desert Dunes, Burnt Orange, Marmalade, Asparagus, and Creme De La Creme

Pieced & Quilted by Erin Grogan

MINI BLOOM PILLOW

Just like the Sprout Wall Hanging, the Mini Bloom Pillow celebrates the hippie flower power movement. Hippies would embroider flowers onto their clothing and wear vibrant colors as a symbol of passive resistance and nonviolence. The Mini Bloom Pillow can bring a pop of vibrant color to your space and hopefully spark joy and peace for you too.

MATERIALS

Yardage is based on 42" (1.1m) wide fabric. Backing assumes at least 4" (10.2cm) coverage on all sides.

Mini Bloom Templates (page 156)

1 Fat Eighth in Fabric A (Red)

1 Fat Eighth in Fabric B (Dark Orange)

1 Fat Eighth in Fabric C (Light Orange)

¼ yard (22.9cm) in Fabric D (Green)

½ yard (45.7cm) in Background (Cream)

½ yard (45.7cm) in backing fabric

½ yard (45.7cm) in backing sleeve fabric

24" x 24" (61 x 61cm) in batting

18" x 18" (45.7 x 45.7cm) pillow insert

CUTTING

All templates include a ¼" (6.4mm) seam allowance.

FROM FABRIC A (RED), CUT:

(2) Template 1

(2) 3" x 4½" (7.6 x 11.4cm) strips

FROM FABRIC B (DARK ORANGE), CUT:

(2) Template 2

(2) 1½" x 4½" (3.8 x 11.4cm) strips

FROM FABRIC C (LIGHT ORANGE), CUT:

(2) Template 3

(2) 2" x 4½" (5.1 x 11.4cm) strips

FROM FABRIC D (GREEN), CUT:

(2) 4½" (11.4cm) x WOF strips, subcut:
(14) Template 5

(1) 1" x 8½" (2.5 x 21.6cm) strip

FROM BACKGROUND (CREAM), CUT:

(4) 5" (12.7cm) x WOF strips, subcut:
(14) Template 4
(14) Template 6

(2) 3" (7.6cm) x WOF strips, subcut:
(2) 3" x 20" (7.6 x 50.8cm) strips
(2) 3" x 16½" (7.6 x 41.9cm) strips

FROM BACKING SLEEVE FABRIC, CUT:

(2) 15" x 20" (38.1 x 50.8cm) rectangles

PIECING BLOCK 1

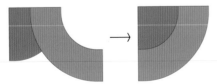

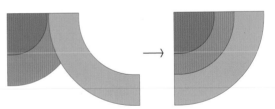

1. Place a Template 2–Fabric B piece, RST, with a Template 1–Fabric A piece as shown. Sew the pieces together, gently nesting the Template 2 piece into the curve of the Template 1 piece. Use the curve method of your choice (pages 9–10). Press toward the Template 2 piece.

2. Place a Template 3–Fabric C piece, RST, with the unit. Sew the pieces together, gently nesting the Template 3 piece into the curve of the unit. Press toward the Template 3 piece.

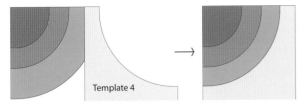

3. Place a Template 4–Background piece, RST, with the unit. Sew the pieces together, gently nesting the Template 4 piece into the curve of the unit. Press toward the Template 4 piece. Square the block to 4½" x 4½" (11.4 x 11.4cm). This is Block 1. Make (2) Block 1s total.

PIECING BLOCK 2

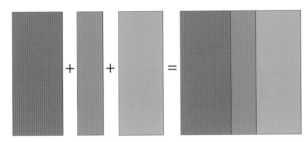

4. Sew together (1) 3" x 4½" (7.6 x 11.4cm) Fabric A strip, (1) 1½" x 4½" (3.8 x 11.4cm) Fabric B strip, and (1) 2" x 4½" (5.1 x 11.4cm) Fabric C strip as shown. Press the seams open. Make (2) strip sets total.

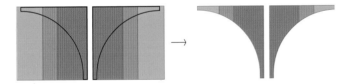

5. Subcut (1) left-facing and (1) right-facing Template 4s from the strip sets as shown. Pay close attention to the template and fabric orientation.

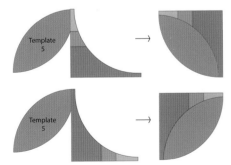

6. Place a Template 4–strip set piece, RST, with a Template 5–Fabric D piece. Sew the pieces together, gently nesting the Template 4 piece into the curve of the Template 5 piece. Press toward the Template 4 piece.

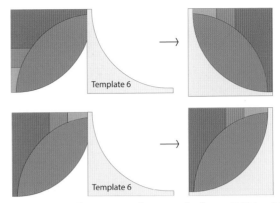

7. Place a Template 6–Background piece, RST, with the unit. Sew the pieces together, gently nesting the Template 6 piece into the curve of the unit. Press toward the Template 6 piece. Square the block to 4½" x 4½" (11.4 x 11.4cm). This is Block 2. Make (2) Block 2s total.

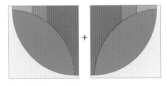

8. With the blocks RST, line up the seams and sew them together as shown. Press the seams open. This will yield (1) unit total.

PIECING THE LEAF BLOCK

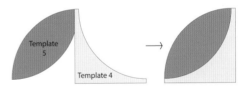

9. Place a Template 4–Background piece, RST, with a Template 5–Fabric D piece as shown. Sew the pieces together, gently nesting the Template 4 piece into the curve of the Template 5 piece. Press toward the Template 4 piece.

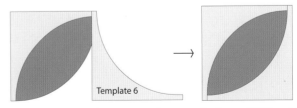

10. Place a Template 6–Background piece, RST, with the unit. Sew the pieces together, gently nesting the Template 6 piece into the curve of the unit. Press toward the Template 6 piece. Square the block to 4½" x 4½" (11.4 x 11.4cm). Make (12) Leaf blocks total.

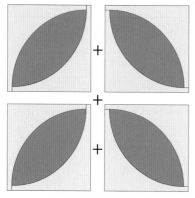

11. Pair (4) Leaf blocks together as shown in the Leaf Assembly Diagram. Sew the blocks together first in rows, then sew the rows together. Press the seams open. Make (2) Leaf units.

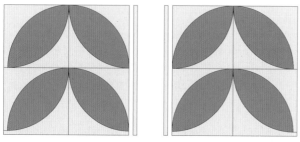

12. Trim ¼" (6.4mm) from the right side of the first Leaf unit and ¼" (6.4mm) from the left side of the second Leaf unit.

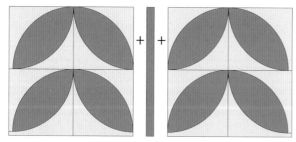

13. Join the (2) units by sewing (1) 1" x 8½" (2.5 x 21.6cm) Fabric D strip between them. Press toward the Fabric D strip. This completes the bottom half of the pillow top.

PILLOW TOP ASSEMBLY

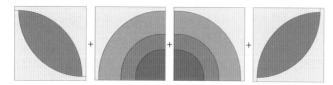

Row 1 Assembly Diagram

14. Sew row 1 of the pillow top using the Row 1 Assembly Diagram. Press the seams open.

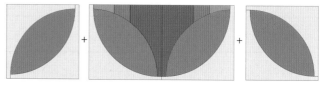

Row 2 Assembly Diagram

15. Sew row 2 of the pillow top using the Row 2 Assembly Diagram. Press the seams open. Join rows 1 and 2 together. This completes the top half of the pillow top.

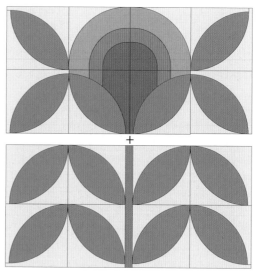

16. Sew together the (2) halves of the pillow top as shown. Press the seams open.

17. Sew (1) 3" x 16½" (7.6 x 41.9cm) Background strip each to the top and to the bottom of the block. Press towards the Background strip.

18. Sew (2) 3" x 20" (7.6 x 50.8cm) Background strips to the sides of the block. Press toward the Background strips. This completes the pillow top, which will be the front.

FINISHING THE PILLOW FRONT

19. Make a three-layer quilt sandwich. Make sure the backing piece is at least 2" (5.1cm) larger all the way around the pillow top. You can use any scrap fabric for this piece as it will be on the inside of the pillow. Quilt as desired, then square the front to 20" x 20" (50.8 x 50.8cm).

PILLOW ENVELOPE SLEEVE ASSEMBLY

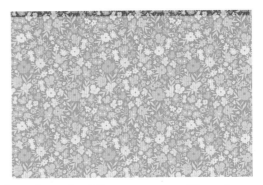

20. Place the 15" x 20" (38.1 x 50.3cm) pillow sleeve fabric wrong side up. Fold over the 15" (38.1cm) edge by ½" (1.3cm) and press. Fold the edge over another ½" (1.3cm) and press again, fully encasing the raw edge. Topstitch the folded-over edge. Make (2) envelope sleeves.

21. Place the (2) envelope sleeves, RST, with the completed pillow top, lining up the raw edges of the sleeves with the raw edges of the pillow top. The folded-over ends will be overlapping in the center of the pillow. Pin in place. Sew around all (4) sides, being sure to backstitch at the beginning and end.

22. Trim off the (4) corners of the pillow, ensuring to not cut into the stitches. This will create sharper points in the finished pillow.

23. Pull the pillow sleeve right side out through the envelope opening. Place the pillow insert inside.

Finished Size: 20" x 20" (50.8 x 50.8cm)

Skill Level: Intermediate

Fabrics Used: Art Gallery Fabrics Pure Solids Cozumel Blue, Blossomed, Burnt Orange, Icy Mint, and Magnetism

Pieced & Quilted by Erin Grogan

CITRUS PILLOW

The Citrus Pillow was inspired by the curves seen in both mid-century modern and Atomic designs. When studying the architecture of this era, you will notice the use of clean, seamless lines and smooth curves. This carried over into artwork, tile, and upholstery design.

MATERIALS

Yardage is based on 42" (1.1m) wide fabric. Backing assumes at least 4" (10.2cm) coverage on all sides.

Citrus Templates (page 145)

1 Fat Quarter in Fabric A (Dark Blue)

1 Fat Quarter in Fabric B (Pink)

1 Fat Quarter in Fabric C (Orange)

1 Fat Quarter in Fabric D (Light Blue)

½ yard (45.7cm) in Background (Gray)

½ yard (45.7cm) in backing fabric

½ yard (45.7cm) in backing sleeve fabric

24" x 24" (61 x 61cm) in batting

18" x 18" (45.7 x 45.7cm) pillow insert

CUTTING

All templates include a ¼" (6.4mm) seam allowance.

FROM FABRIC A (DARK BLUE), CUT:

(3) Template 2

(3) Template 3

(1) 4½" x 4½" (11.4 x 11.4cm) square

FROM FABRIC B (PINK), CUT:

(3) Template 2

(3) Template 3

(1) 4½" x 4½" (11.4 x 11.4cm) square

FROM FABRIC C (ORANGE), CUT:

(3) Template 2

(3) Template 3

(1) 4½" x 4½" (11.4 x 11.4cm) square

FROM FABRIC D (LIGHT BLUE), CUT:

(3) Template 2

(3) Template 3

(1) 4½" x 4½" (11.4 x 11.4cm) square

FROM BACKGROUND (GRAY), CUT:

(2) 4½" (11.4cm) x WOF strips, subcut:
(12) Template 1

(2) 3½" x 16½" (8.9 x 41.9cm) strips

(2) 3" x 20" (7.6 x 50.8cm) strips

FROM BACKING SLEEVE FABRIC, CUT:

(2) 15" x 20" (38.1 x 50.8cm) rectangles

PIECING THE ORANGE PEEL BLOCK

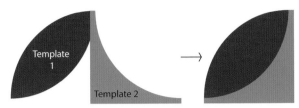

1. Place a Template 2 piece, RST, with a Template 1 piece as shown. Sew the pieces together, gently nesting the Template 2 piece into the curve of the Template 1 piece. Press toward the Template 2 piece.

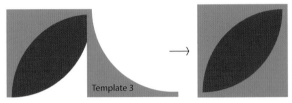

2. Place a Template 3 piece, RST, with the unit. Sew the pieces together, gently nesting the Template 3 piece into the curve of the unit. Press toward the Template 3 piece. Trim the block to 4½" x 4½" (11.4 x 11.4cm) square. Make (12) Orange Peel blocks according to the colors in the Orange Peel Chart.

ORANGE PEEL CHART

Template 2 & 3 Color	Block Qty
Fabric A	3
Fabric B	3
Fabric C	3
Fabric D	3

PILLOW TOP ASSEMBLY

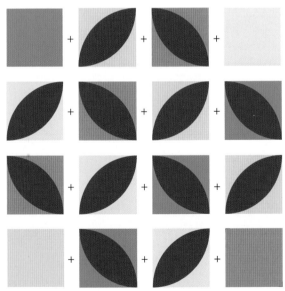

3. Arrange the (12) Orange Peel blocks into rows according to the diagram. Place a 4½" x 4½" (11.4 x 11.4cm) square of each color in the corners. Sew together the blocks into rows. Press the seams open.

4. Sew (1) 3½" x 16½" (8.9 x 41.9cm) Background strip each to the top and bottom of the block. Press toward the Background strip.

5. Sew (2) 3" x 20" (7.6 x 50.8cm) Background strips to the sides of the block. Press toward the Background strip. This completes the pillow top, which will be the front.

FINISHING THE PILLOW FRONT

6. Make a three-layer quilt sandwich. Make sure the backing piece is at least 2" (5.1cm) larger all the way around the pillow top. You can use any scrap fabric for this piece as it will be on the inside of the pillow. Quilt as desired, then square the front to 20" x 20" (50.8 x 50.8cm).

PILLOW ENVELOPE SLEEVE ASSEMBLY

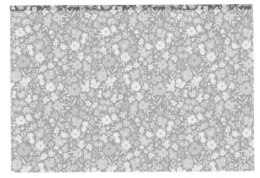

7. Place the 15" x 20" (38.1 x 50.3cm) pillow sleeve fabric wrong side up. Fold over the 15" (38.1cm) edge by ½" (1.3cm) and press. Fold the edge over another ½" (1.3cm) and press again, fully encasing the raw edge. Topstitch the folded-over edge. Make (2) envelope sleeves.

8. Place the (2) envelope sleeves, RST, with the completed pillow top, lining up the raw edges of the sleeves with the raw edges of the pillow top. The folded-over ends will be overlapping in the center of the pillow. Pin in place. Sew around all (4) sides, being sure to backstitch at the beginning and end.

9. Trim off the (4) corners of the pillow, ensuring to not cut into the stitches. This will create sharper points in the finished pillow.

10. Pull the pillow sleeve right side out through the envelope opening. Place the pillow insert inside.

TEMPLATES

Photocopy and enlarge these templates shown on pages 130–156 by 200%.
You can also download the full-size template files by following the QR code
or going to the website: foxpatterns.com/retro-curved-pieced-quilts/

RAINBOW SNAIL TEMPLATES

PHOTOCOPY 200%

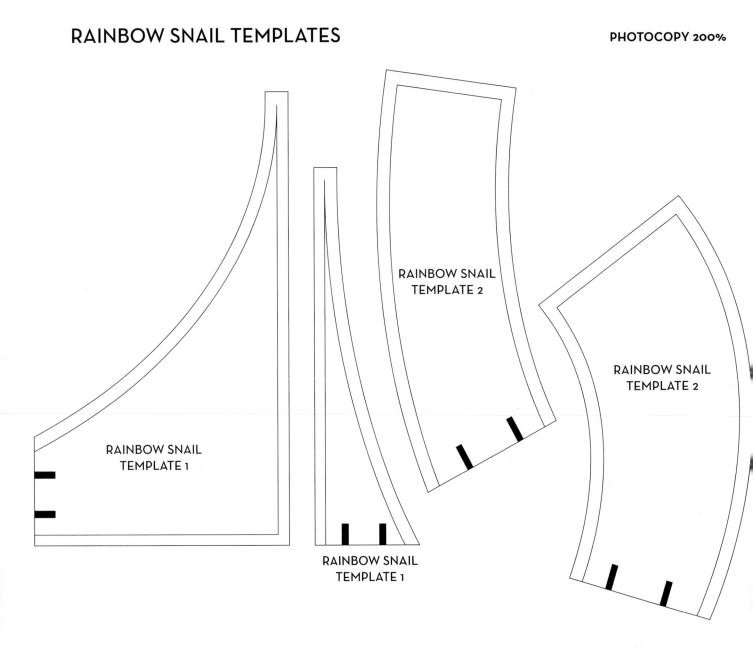

RAINBOW SNAIL
TEMPLATE 2

RAINBOW SNAIL
TEMPLATE 2

RAINBOW SNAIL
TEMPLATE 1

RAINBOW SNAIL
TEMPLATE 1

RAINBOW SNAIL TEMPLATES

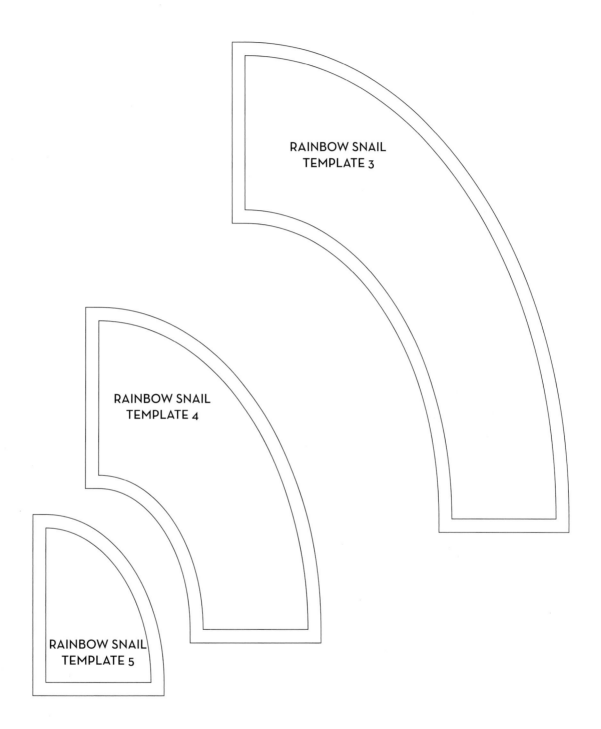

RAINBOW SNAIL
TEMPLATE 3

RAINBOW SNAIL
TEMPLATE 4

RAINBOW SNAIL
TEMPLATE 5

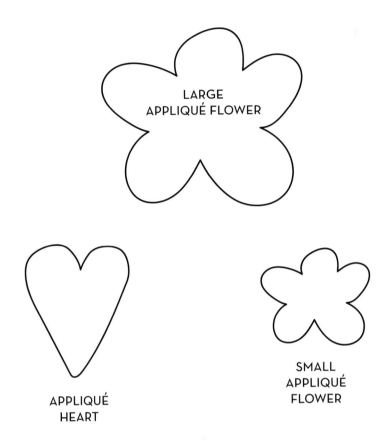

LARGE
APPLIQUÉ FLOWER

APPLIQUÉ
HEART

SMALL
APPLIQUÉ
FLOWER

SMALL APPLIQUÉ
CENTER

LARGE APPLIQUÉ
CENTER

PEACE, LOVE & PATCHWORK TEMPLATES

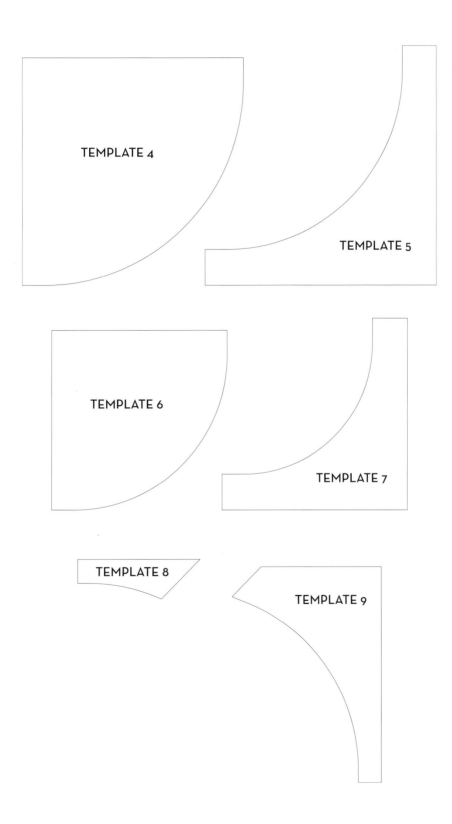

TEMPLATE 4

TEMPLATE 5

TEMPLATE 6

TEMPLATE 7

TEMPLATE 8

TEMPLATE 9

PEACE, LOVE & PATCHWORK PEACE SIGN TEMPLATE

Print all 12 sections. Tape the pieces together in a 3x4 grid for Templates 1, 2, and 3.

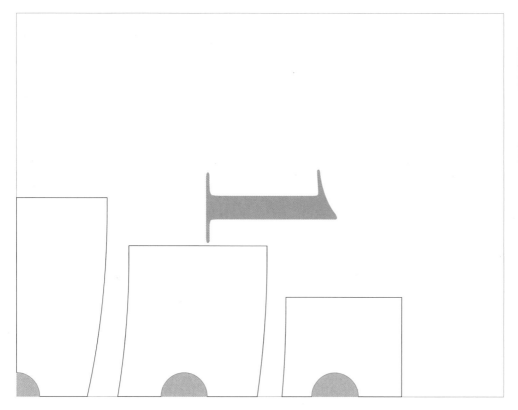

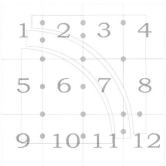

TEMPLATE 4 LOOKS LIKE ABOVE WHEN ASSEMBLED

PEACE, LOVE & PATCHWORK PEACE SIGN TEMPLATE

PHOTOCOPY 200%

Print all 12 sections. Tape the pieces together in a 3x4 grid for Templates 1, 2, and 3.

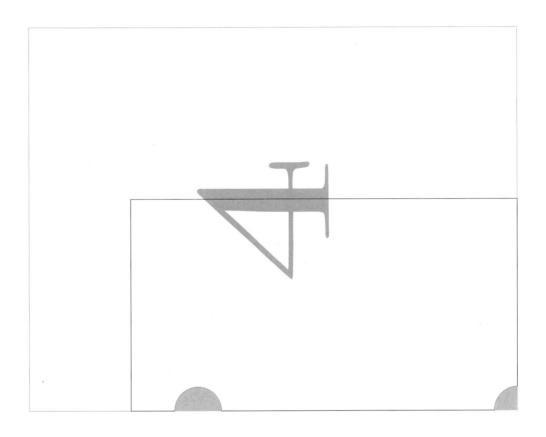

PEACE, LOVE & PATCHWORK PEACE SIGN TEMPLATE

PHOTOCOPY 200%

Print all 12 sections. Tape the pieces together in a 3x4 grid for Templates 1, 2, and 3.

PEACE, LOVE & PATCHWORK PEACE SIGN TEMPLATE

PHOTOCOPY 200%

Print all 12 sections. Tape the pieces together in a 3x4 grid for Templates 1, 2, and 3.

PEACE, LOVE & PATCHWORK PEACE SIGN TEMPLATE

PHOTOCOPY 200%

Print all 12 sections. Tape the pieces together in a 3x4 grid for Templates 1, 2, and 3.

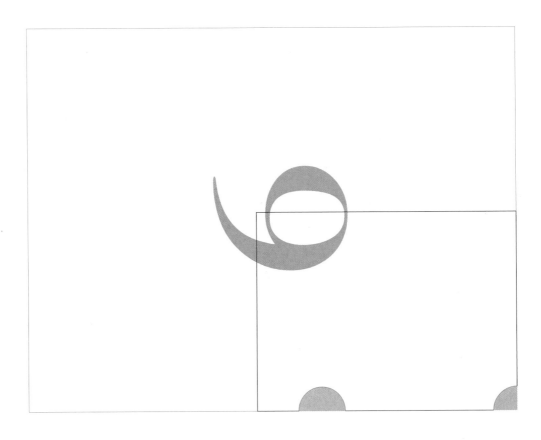

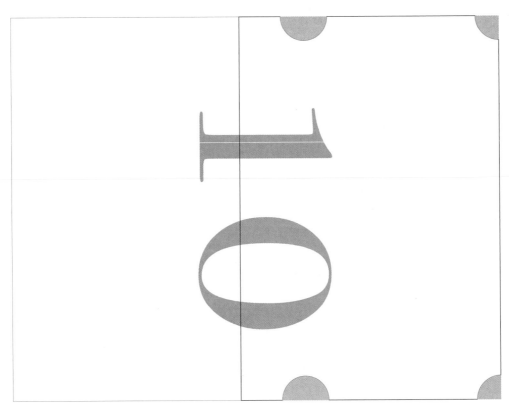

PEACE, LOVE & PATCHWORK PEACE SIGN TEMPLATE   PHOTOCOPY 200%

Print all 12 sections. Tape the pieces together in a 3x4 grid for Templates 1, 2, and 3.

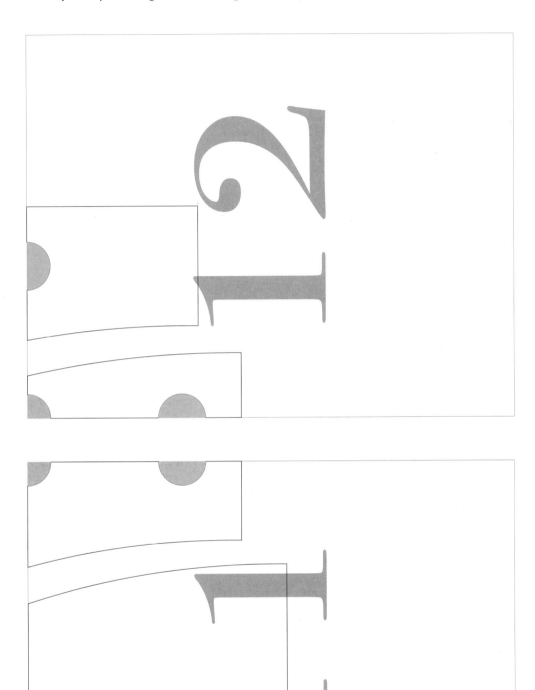

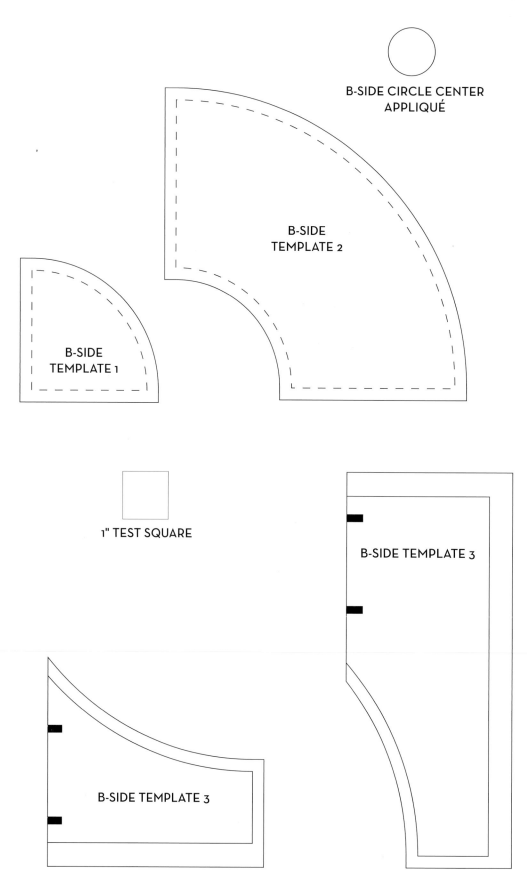

B-SIDE CIRCLE CENTER
APPLIQUÉ

B-SIDE
TEMPLATE 2

B-SIDE
TEMPLATE 1

1" TEST SQUARE

B-SIDE TEMPLATE 3

B-SIDE TEMPLATE 3

DARLING DAISIES TEMPLATES

PHOTOCOPY 200%

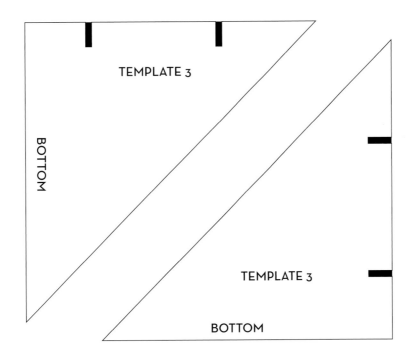

TEMPLATE 3

BOTTOM

TEMPLATE 3

BOTTOM

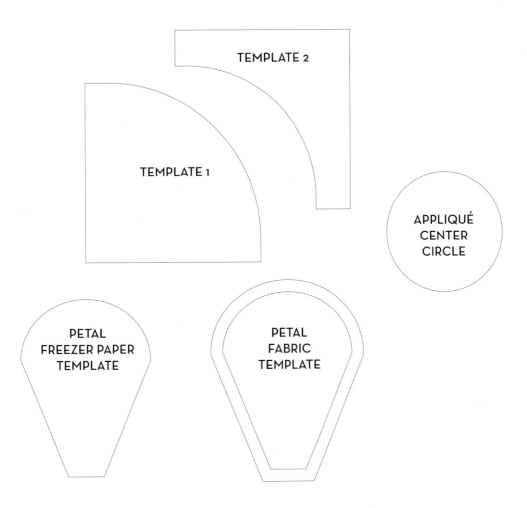

TEMPLATE 2

TEMPLATE 1

APPLIQUÉ
CENTER
CIRCLE

PETAL
FREEZER PAPER
TEMPLATE

PETAL
FABRIC
TEMPLATE

DOUBLE RAINBOW TEMPLATES

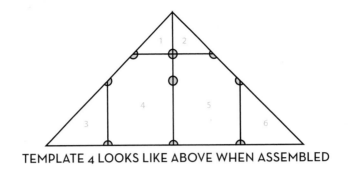

TEMPLATE 4 LOOKS LIKE ABOVE WHEN ASSEMBLED

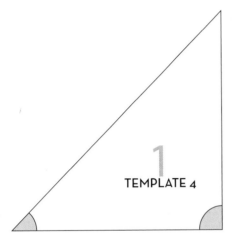

1

TEMPLATE 4

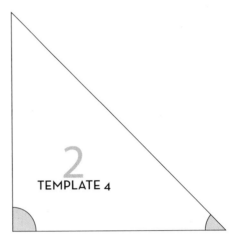

2

TEMPLATE 4

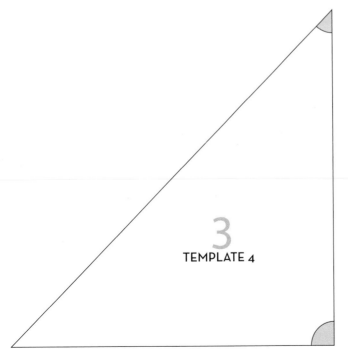

3

TEMPLATE 4

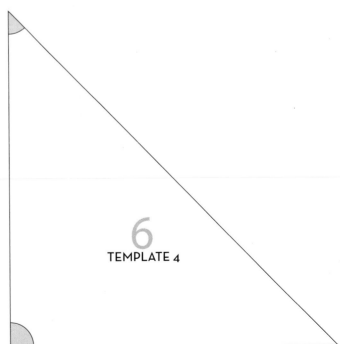

6

TEMPLATE 4

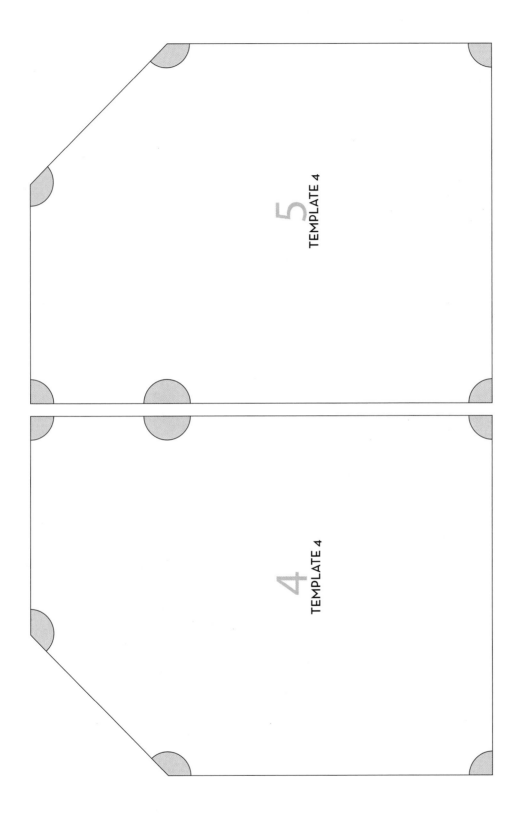

5
TEMPLATE 4

4
TEMPLATE 4

DOUBLE RAINBOW TEMPLATES

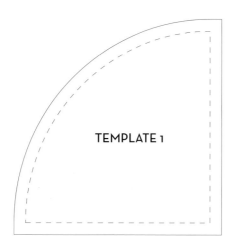

TEMPLATE 1

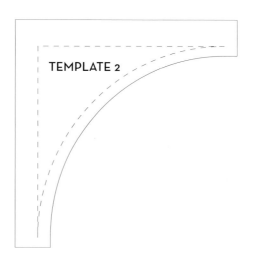

TEMPLATE 2

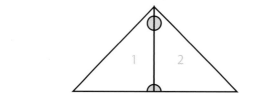

TEMPLATE 3 LOOKS LIKE ABOVE WHEN ASSEMBLED

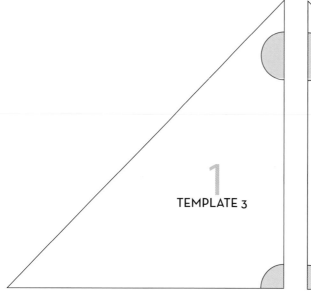

1

TEMPLATE 3

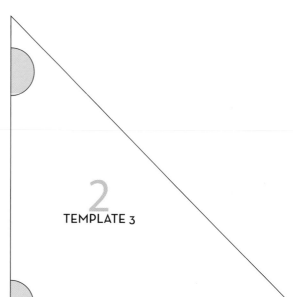

2

TEMPLATE 3

MARVELOUS MUSHROOMS TEMPLATES

PHOTOCOPY 200%

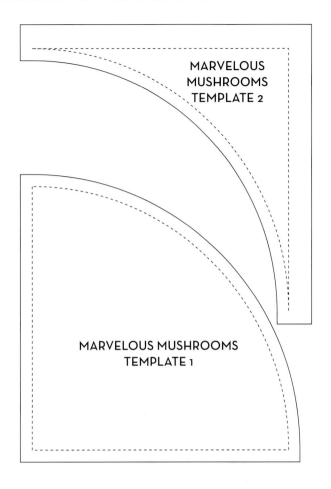

MARVELOUS
MUSHROOMS
TEMPLATE 2

MARVELOUS MUSHROOMS
TEMPLATE 1

CITRUS TEMPLATES

PHOTOCOPY 200%

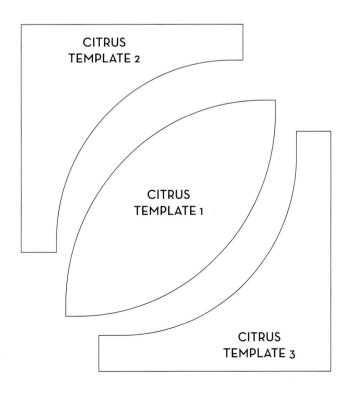

CITRUS
TEMPLATE 2

CITRUS
TEMPLATE 1

CITRUS
TEMPLATE 3

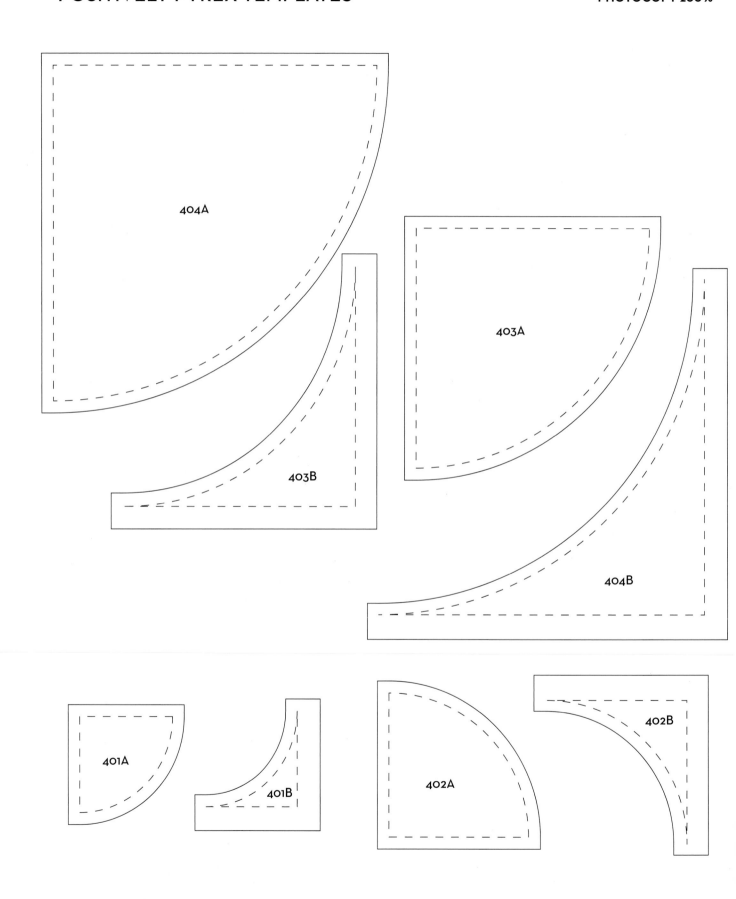

404A

403B

403A

404B

401A

401B

402A

402B

POSITIVELY PYREX TEMPLATES

PHOTOCOPY 200%

POSITIVELY PYREX
FULL BLOOM TEMPLATES

POSITIVELY PYREX SPROUT TEMPLATES

POSITIVELY PYREX
CRAZY DAISIES TEMPLATES

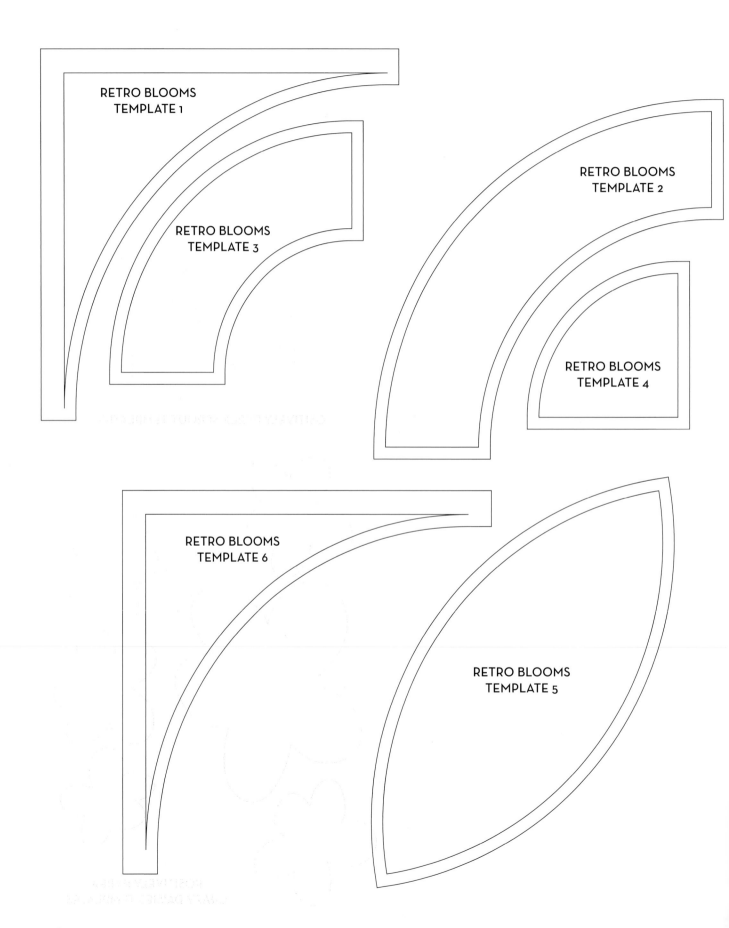

RETRO BLOOMS
TEMPLATE 1

RETRO BLOOMS
TEMPLATE 3

RETRO BLOOMS
TEMPLATE 2

RETRO BLOOMS
TEMPLATE 4

RETRO BLOOMS
TEMPLATE 6

RETRO BLOOMS
TEMPLATE 5

STRAWBERRY FIELDS TEMPLATES

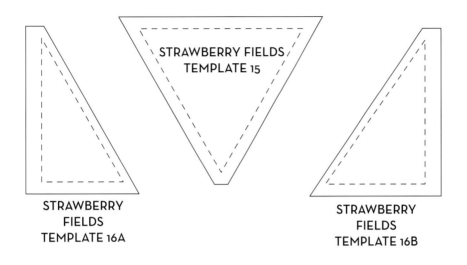

STRAWBERRY FIELDS
TEMPLATE 15

STRAWBERRY
FIELDS
TEMPLATE 16A

STRAWBERRY
FIELDS
TEMPLATE 16B

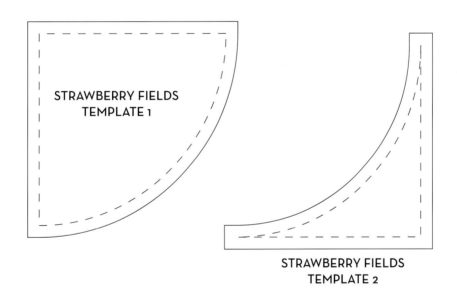

STRAWBERRY FIELDS
TEMPLATE 1

STRAWBERRY FIELDS
TEMPLATE 2

STRAWBERRY FIELDS TEMPLATE

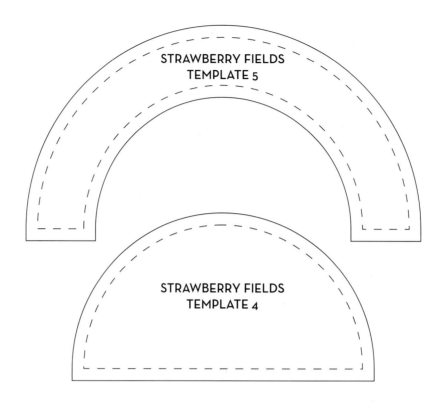

STRAWBERRY FIELDS
TEMPLATE 5

STRAWBERRY FIELDS
TEMPLATE 4

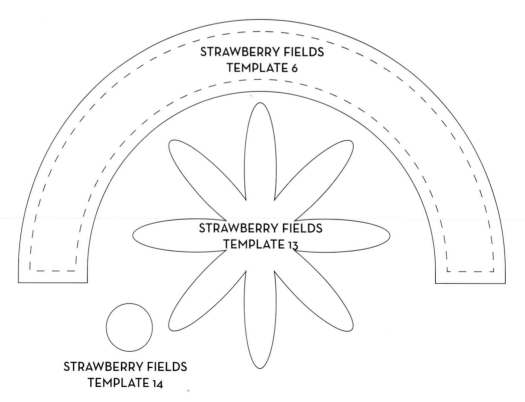

STRAWBERRY FIELDS
TEMPLATE 6

STRAWBERRY FIELDS
TEMPLATE 13

STRAWBERRY FIELDS
TEMPLATE 14

STRAWBERRY FIELDS TEMPLATE

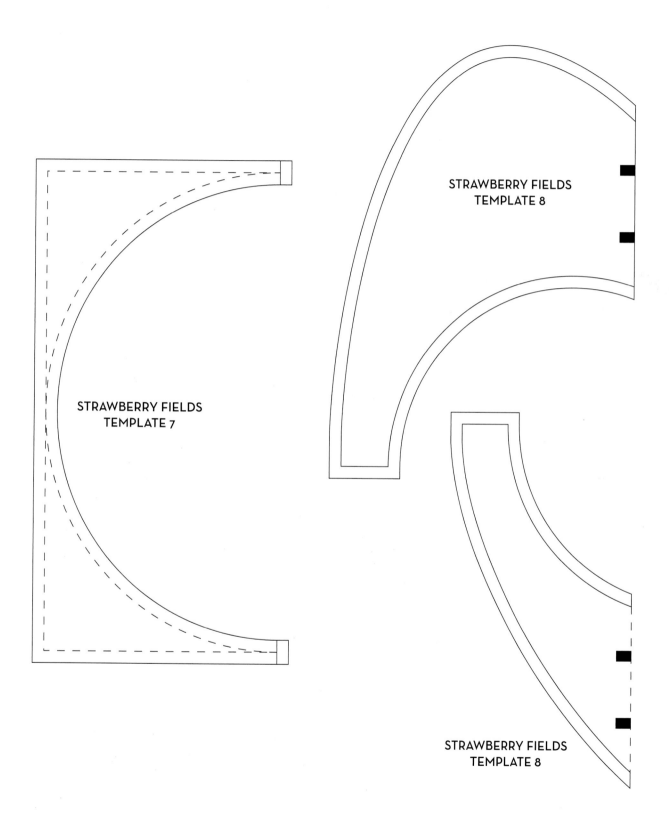

STRAWBERRY FIELDS
TEMPLATE 8

STRAWBERRY FIELDS
TEMPLATE 7

STRAWBERRY FIELDS
TEMPLATE 8

STRAWBERRY FIELDS TEMPLATES

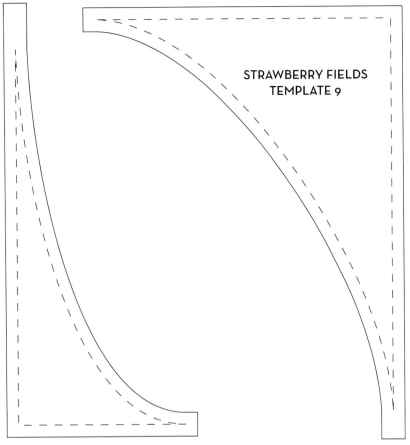

STRAWBERRY FIELDS
TEMPLATE 9

STRAWBERRY FIELDS
TEMPLATE 10

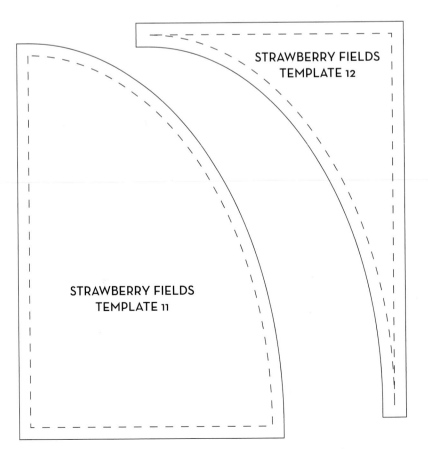

STRAWBERRY FIELDS
TEMPLATE 12

STRAWBERRY FIELDS
TEMPLATE 11

SO MOD TEMPLATES

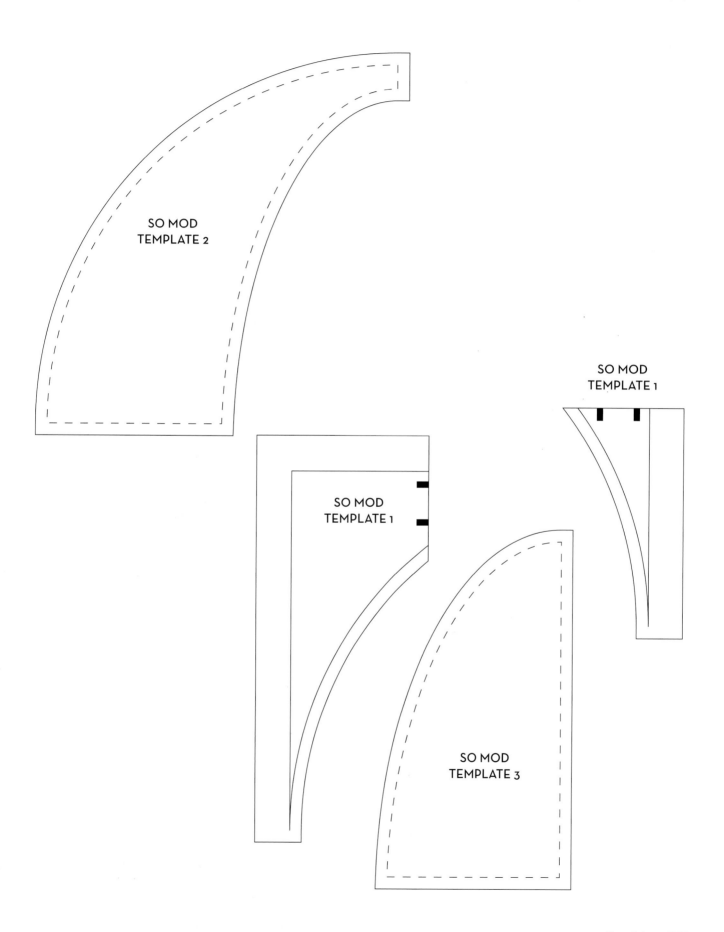

SO MOD
TEMPLATE 2

SO MOD
TEMPLATE 1

SO MOD
TEMPLATE 1

SO MOD
TEMPLATE 3

RETRO STARS TEMPLATES

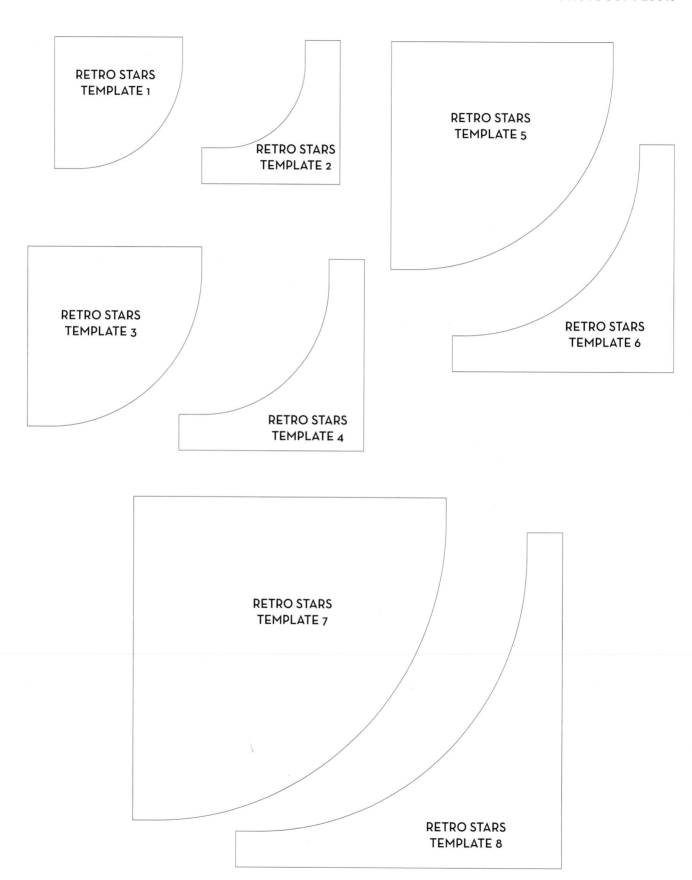

RETRO STARS
TEMPLATE 1

RETRO STARS
TEMPLATE 2

RETRO STARS
TEMPLATE 5

RETRO STARS
TEMPLATE 3

RETRO STARS
TEMPLATE 6

RETRO STARS
TEMPLATE 4

RETRO STARS
TEMPLATE 7

RETRO STARS
TEMPLATE 8

SETTING SUN TEMPLATES

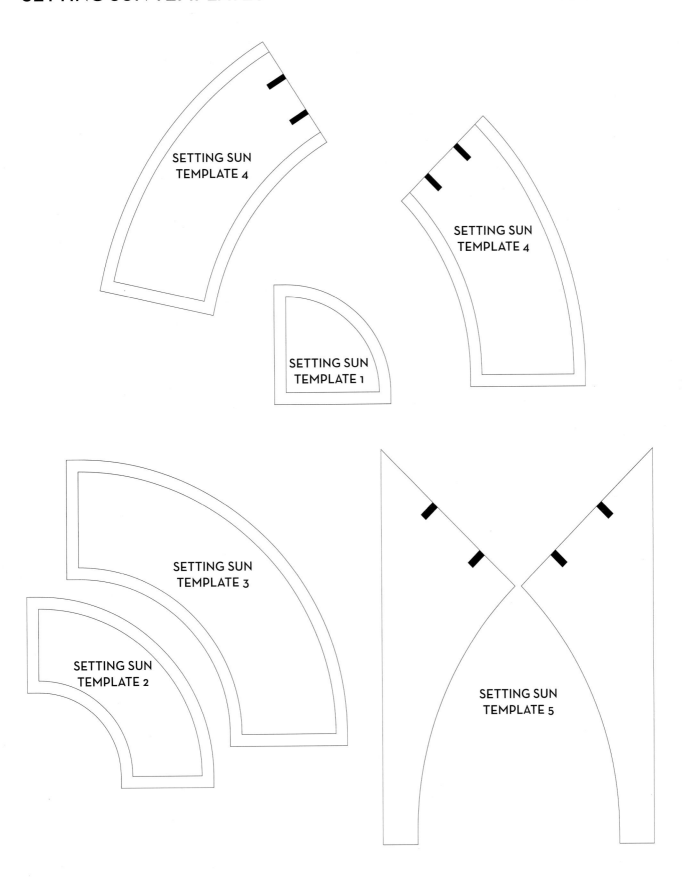

SETTING SUN
TEMPLATE 4

SETTING SUN
TEMPLATE 4

SETTING SUN
TEMPLATE 1

SETTING SUN
TEMPLATE 3

SETTING SUN
TEMPLATE 2

SETTING SUN
TEMPLATE 5

MINI BLOOM TEMPLATES

PHOTOCOPY 200%

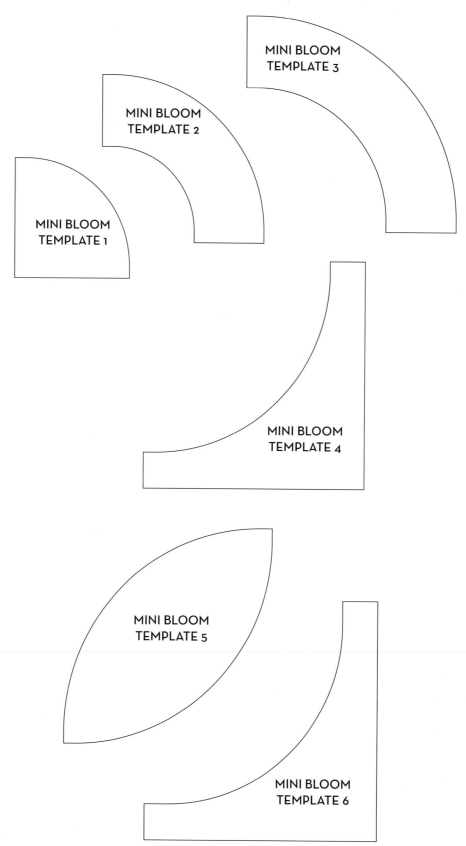

MINI BLOOM
TEMPLATE 3

MINI BLOOM
TEMPLATE 2

MINI BLOOM
TEMPLATE 1

MINI BLOOM
TEMPLATE 4

MINI BLOOM
TEMPLATE 5

MINI BLOOM
TEMPLATE 6

ABOUT THE AUTHOR

Erin Grogan, the pattern designer and founder of Love Sew Modern, was introduced to sewing by her grandmother, Eleanor, who was a professional seamstress. As a child she would fill a notebook with fashion designs with the dream of one day becoming a clothing designer. Working alongside her grandmother, they would make her designs together. These precious moments sparked her love for sewing and design.

In 2017, Erin took her first trip to a modern quilt shop. Surrounded by all the bright, bold fabrics and modern quilts, she knew in that moment she wanted to become a quilter. In January 2020, Erin left her corporate job to focus on growing her dream of becoming a quilt pattern designer and educator. She founded her company, Love Sew Modern, and has since been published in many quilting books and magazines.

Her modern designs are inspired by traditionalism and evoke feelings of nostalgia. She continues to look for opportunities to make her mark on the quilting community, including teaching the next generation how to sew and quilt. To learn more about Erin and see her work, visit www.LoveSewModern.com or find her on all social media platforms @LoveSewModern.

ACKNOWLEDGMENTS

The past year of putting this book together has been the realization of one of my biggest dreams. I feel as though I've poured my heart and soul into each design and really stepped outside my comfort zone to bring something magical to life. None of this would have been possible without some of the amazing people who supported me.

Firstly, I'd like to thank my husband and children who understood and allowed me to bring my work with me for every moment in our lives this past year. I wrote the pages in our hotel room during family vacations. I hand-quilted during soccer practices and long car rides. You are always my number one cheerleaders, and I couldn't have asked for a better support system. I love you three so very much.

If you've been quilting for a while, you know the quality of your tools and fabric make a huge difference in the quality and longevity of your quilts. I was beyond blessed when Art Gallery Fabrics agreed to sponsor this book and supplied me with all the fabrics needed to make all 15 projects. I knew Art Gallery Pure Solids were the only fabrics I would need for this book. Their dusty color palette was a perfect match for my retro flair. Also, when thinking about the techniques used in these patterns, from raw edge appliqué and sewing curves, I knew their higher thread count and minimal-to-no fraying fabrics were the right ones for the job. I'd personally like to thank Pat Bravo, Walter Bravo, and Marcela Loayza at Art Gallery Fabrics for believing in me, inspiring me, and supporting me through this process. You're all some of the kindest people I've had the pleasure of getting to know in the quilting industry and I'm sending a hug to you all in Florida.

To Kelly Stauffer, there are not enough thank yous I could possibly say. You have been an amazing friend and colleague who has kept me organized and on schedule while creating this book. You were my right hand in helping me to sew together so many of these quilts. You are a prolific quilter, and I'm lucky to call you my friend.

To Megan Saenz, thank you so much for helping to bring my mid-century modern vision to life and helping me to capture my quilts so beautifully. Your photography is so light and airy, and I really appreciate what you do!

To Mickie Gelling and Tami Pugmire, thank you so much for stitching out beautiful edge-to-edge designs on some of my quilts. You both did beautiful jobs and were an important asset to me being able to get everything done on time.

To my grandmother, Eleanor McGonagall, who taught me the beauty and power of sewing as a young girl. Every time I sit down at my sewing machine, I think of you and know you're with me. Although you never got to see my quilts, I like to believe I would have made you proud. I love you so much and wish you were here to see what I've created.

Lastly, I want to say a special thank you to my friend and mentor Elizabeth Chappell. Thank you for encouraging me to follow my dreams from the very beginning. You were one of the first people to believe in me and I will be forever thankful.

INDEX

A

appliqué, raw edge, 11

B

bias (definition), 9
big stitch quilting, 16
  tips for, 16, 17
blocks
  Bloom block, 79, 116
  Circle block, 90
  Covered Corner block, 37, 40
  curved blocks, squaring up, 11
  Daisy Dresden block, 12, 45
  Dresden block, 45
  Drunkard's Path block, 8, 45, 51,
    60, 70, 104, 111
  Economy block, 38, 61
  Flower block, 65
  Flying Geese block, 37, 40, 56, 87
  Hourglass block, 39
  Leaf block, 91, 121
  Nine Patch block, 63, 65
  Orange Peel block, 127
  Owl block, 90–92
  Record block, 40
  Sawtooth Star block, 104
  Strawberry block, 87
  Sun block, 111
Bloom block, 79, 116
B-Side Quilt, 34
  templates, 140
butterfly, piecing, 30

C

Circle block, 90
Citrus Pillow, 124
  templates, 145
concave curve (definition), 8
convex curve (definition), 8
Covered Corner block, 37, 40
curved blocks, squaring up, 11

curves, how to sew, 8
  glue pen method, 10
  no-pin method, 10
  pinning method, 9
cutting mat, self healing, 5

D

Daisy Dresden block, 12, 45
Darling Daisies Quilt, 42
  templates, 141
decorative stitching presser foot, 5
Double Rainbow Quilt, 48
  templates, 142–144
Dresden block, 45
Drunkard's Path block, 8, 45, 51, 60, 70,
  104, 111

E

Economy block, 38, 61

F

fabric scissors, 7
Flower block, 65
Flying Geese block, 37, 40, 56, 87
freezer paper, 7
FriXion pen, 7
fusible, 7

G

glue pen method (sewing curves), 10
glue pen, 7
grain (definition), 8

H

half-rectangle triangle, 62
half-square triangle, 39
Hourglass block, 39
HRT, 62
HST, 39, 57, 86

I

iron, 7

L

Leaf block, 91, 121

M

marking tool, 7
Marvelous Mushrooms Quilt, 54
  templates, 145
Mini Bloom Pillow, 118
  templates, 156

N

Nine Patch block, 63, 65
no-pin method (sewing curves), 10

O

Orange Peel block, 127
Owl block, 90–92

P

peace sign, piecing, 29
Peace, Love, and Patchwork Quilt, 26
  templates, 132–139
pillow
  Citrus Pillow, 124
  Mini Bloom Pillow, 118
pillow envelope sleeve assembly, 123,
  128
pinning method (sewing curves), 9
pins, 7
Positively Pyrex Quilt, 68
  templates, 146–147
presser foot, 5
  decorative stitching, 5
projects
  B-Side Quilt, 34
  Citrus Pillow, 124
  Darling Daisies Quilt, 42
  Double Rainbow Quilt, 48
  Marvelous Mushrooms Quilt, 54
  Mini Bloom Pillow, 118
  Peace, Love, and Patchwork
    Quilt, 26
  Positively Pyrex Quilt, 68

Rainbow Snails Quilt, 20
Retro Blooms Quilt, 76
Retro Stars Quilt, 100
Setting Sun Wall Hanging, 108
So Mod Quilt, 94
Sprout Wall Hanging, 112
Strawberry Fields Quilt, 82
Pyrex, 4

Q

quilt
B-Side Quilt, 34
Darling Daisies Quilt, 42
Double Rainbow Quilt, 48
Marvelous Mushrooms Quilt, 54
Peace, Love, and Patchwork
Quilt, 26
Positively Pyrex Quilt, 68
Rainbow Snails Quilt, 20
Retro Blooms Quilt, 76
Retro Stars Quilt, 100
So Mod Quilt, 94
Strawberry Fields Quilt, 82
quilting ruler, 7

R

Rainbow Snails Quilt, 20
templates, 130–131
raw edge appliqué, 11
Record block, 40
Retro Blooms Quilt, 76
templates, 148
Retro Stars Quilt, 100
templates, 154
right sides together (definition), 8
rotary cutter, 5
RST (definition), 8

S

Sawtooth Star block, 104
seam ripper, 7
Setting Sun Wall Hanging, 108
templates, 155
sewing machine, 5
So Mod Quilt, 94
templates, 153
Sprout Wall Hanging, 112
squaring up curved blocks, 11
starch, 7

Strawberry block, 87
Strawberry Fields Quilt, 82
templates, 149–152
Sun block, 111

T

template, 7
thread, 5
8wt, 5
12wt, 5
50wt, 5

W

wall hanging
Setting Sun Wall Hanging, 108
Sprout Wall Hanging, 112
warp (definition), 8
weft (definition), 8